libraries

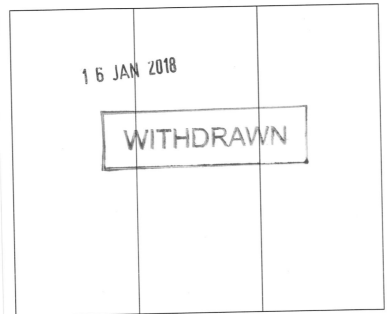

Glasgow
CITY COUNCIL

P'S

RA RIE

SEARCH PRESS

PROGGY'S
RAG RUG MENAGERIE

20 SOFT AND SNUGGLY ANIMALS TO HOOK AND SEW

HAYLEY SMITH
Founder of Craft Yourself Silly

First published in Great Britain in 2017
by Search Press Limited
Wellwood, North Farm Road,
Tunbridge Wells, Kent TN2 3DR

ISBN: 978-1-78221-554-7

Project Editor: Julie Brooke
Proofreader: Cassie Armstrong
Designer: Leah Germann
Cover design: Leah Germann
Cover photo: Craft Yourself Silly
Print ISBN: 978-1-68099-337-0
Ebook ISBN: 978-1-68099-338-7

Printed in China

Contents

Introduction 6

Woodland Creatures 8

Friendly Fox 10
Big Bold Badger 14
Happy Hedgehog 18
Sassy Squirrel 22

Farmyard Favourites 26

Little Lamb 28
Pink Pig 32
Spooky Bat 36
Fluffy Duck 40

Perfect Pets 44

Cuddly Kitten 46
Darling Puppy 50
Floppy Bunny 54
Tiny Tortoise 58

Feathered Friends 62

Pretty Parrot 64
Wise Old Owl 68
Rockin' Robin 72
Baby Penguin 76

Water Babies 80

Cute Clown Fish 82
Snuggly Seal 86
Flappy Turtle 90
Crazy Frog 94

Before you start 98
Resources 107
Templates 108
Index 128
Acknowledgements 128

Introduction

'Proggy' is the colloquial term used in the northeast of England – the area where I was born and live and work today – for a rag rug. But, depending where you travel in the UK, you'll find many names for the same technique: 'clippy', 'hooky', 'proddy', and many, many more.

I discovered the technique while running a pancake café and pottery painting studio with my mother. We saw a big resurgence in interest for learning traditional craft skills, and one of the things we were asked was how to make rag rugs. I taught myself the basics, and once I realised how simple the proggy technique was, I saw it had the potential to be used for more than just the humble rug.

Until the mid-twentieth century, a proggy mat was a staple in the Northumberland home. Traditionally created from old clothes, making the mat was an annual event, recycling and reusing fabrics long before it was fashionable. The newly made mat went onto the bed to keep your toes warm and toasty during cold Northumberland nights. The one that used to be on the bed went onto the bedroom floor, and the old rugs then cascaded down the pecking order, with the oldest ones being used in the scullery.

The strips for the rug were traditionally cut out using the side of a matchbox as a guide to keep them all the same size, and potato sacks were used for the backing. The fabrics used were old woollen coats in blacks, browns, greys and blues. Today, these heavy, cumbersome fabrics have been replaced with lighter materials in a rainbow of colours. And it is not just the colours you can experiment with. Modern fabrics such as fleece are lightweight, which means you can make proggy bags and soft toys that are soft and easy to carry, as well as wall hangings, cushions, bags, throws and even clothes.

My first proggy project was Graham the Hedgehog – how could I not?
His spikes were just the perfect partner for the proggy technique. We
then launched Proggy® rag rug kits on a television shopping channel,
and were overwhelmed by the positive response that we had for the craft.
At that point Craft Yourself Silly was born, and it became a company in its
own right, specialising in fabric crafts.

The next additions to our Proggy® family were Alan the Owl and Bill the
Badger, inspired by the men who worked in the office next door. From then
on, all of the creatures in our kits have been named after friends and family
who have been involved in our Proggy® journey. The collection has expanded
to include more than thirty soft toys, a Christmas and Halloween range, lots
of interior design projects and a variety of bags.

Proggy® launched in the United States in 2015 to an amazing reception and
won regional and national export awards. Proggy® products now appear all
over the world, and we are proud to have taken a local, traditional craft and
created a fun and friendly product that is available to a global market.

We hope you enjoy the projects in this book as much as we have.

HAYLEY SMITH

Woodland Creatures

As night falls in the woods, fox, badger and hedgehog emerge from their burrows to search for food. As the busy part of their day begins, the squirrel's search for nuts and leaves comes to an end and he nestles down to sleep.

Friendly Fox

This little fellow is always making mischief, wagging his bushy orange tail, poking his pointy nose into everyone's business. You cannot help but love him.

You will need

50 x 50cm (20 x 20in) hessian

100 x 50cm (40 x 20in) orange fleece

100 x 50cm (40 x 20in) white fleece

15 x 15cm (6 x 6in) black fleece

one pair 12mm (½in) black safety eyes

one 12mm (½in) black safety nose

250g (10oz) polyester soft toy stuffing

orange or white sewing thread

fabric marker pen

scissors

ruler

pointed rag rug tool (see page 98)

sewing needle

fabric glue (optional)

Difficulty rating

Intermediate

Completed size

20cm high x 13cm wide x 13cm deep
(8in high x 5in wide x 5in deep)

Prepare the pieces

1 Using the templates on page 108, cut out the body and tail sections from hessian and copy the markings. Cut out two ears, the snout and feet from black, white and orange fleece as directed on the templates. Cut a strip measuring 1.5 x 25cm (½ x 10in) from the orange fleece; this will be used to attach the tail to the body. Cut the remaining orange and white fleece into 1.5 x 5cm (½ x 2in) strips (see Proggy strip template on page 101).

Hook the pieces

2 For the front of the body, fold the hessian along the marked lines, and use the technique shown on page 102 to secure the fold. Fill in the outline of the body using the technique shown on page 102. Continue until the folded edge is secure. Repeat for the back of the body and the tail, adding in the tummy section and the tip of the tail in white. Once the outline is complete, trim any excess hessian using scissors.

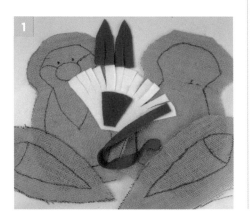

Add the eyes and ears

3 Attach the safety eyes in the positions marked on the template using the technique on page 105.

4 To add the ears, push the two strips of fabric at the base of one ear through the hessian on one side of the head as marked on the template, then tie them together using the technique on page 105. Keep the strips three strands of hessian apart. Repeat on the other side of the head.

Adding the snout

5 Stab stitch the orange snout section onto the white snout section, positioning it as shown on the template. Green thread is used in the photograph to show the stitches.

6 Fold the snout in half so that the orange section is on the inside and backstitch the straight edges together, leaving a small gap at the tip and the seam allowance shown on the template. Turn the snout right side out and insert the safety nose through the hole in the tip, using the same technique as for the eyes.

7 Fill in the body and tail sections using the technique shown on page 102. Do not fill in the section where the snout will sit.

8 To attach the snout, align the centre of the snout with the corresponding section of the hessian. Push four strips of fabric from the snout (one each for the top, bottom, left and right) through the hessian and adjust until you are happy with the positioning. Push through the remaining strips and tie together in pairs using double knots. Secure with fabric glue if desired.

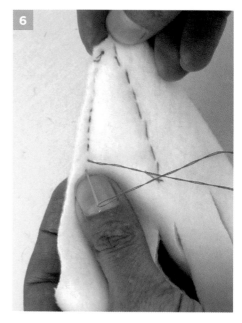

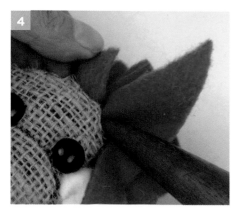

Add the tail

9 For the tail, fold the strip of orange fleece in half (shown here in black) and push both ends through the base of one of the tail sections hooked in step 2. Work from the wrong to the right side, and insert them three strands of hessian apart. Hold the tail sections with wrong sides facing each other and oversew together, adding stuffing as you go.

10 Position the tail on the body and insert the fabric strips through the hessian, three strands apart. Tie the ends together using a double knot. Secure with fabric glue if desired.

Complete the fox

11 Put the front and back body pieces together with the wrong sides facing each other. Starting at the bottom, sew the pieces together, leaving a gap large enough to push the stuffing through. Stuff the body, then oversew the opening closed.

12 Position the feet section at the base of the body and push the feet through the hessian, using the pointed tool. Oversew the feet to the edge of the hessian sections. If necessary, use scissors to trim the fleece covering the fox body so it is a uniform length.

Try This!

T-shirt texture

Try using T-shirt fabric for this project – the edges of the strips will roll together as you work to create a furry texture.

Big Bold Badger

Foraging for bugs in the dead of night is where you would most often find this inquisitive chap, but his striped snout loves a good hug too.

You will need

100 x 50cm (40 x 20in) hessian

150 x 50cm (60 x 20in) grey fleece

25 x 25cm (10 x 10in) white fleece

20 x 12cm (8 x 5in) black fleece

one pair 12mm (½in) black safety eyes

250g (10oz) polyester soft toy stuffing

black or white sewing thread

fabric marker pen

scissors

ruler

pointed rag rug tool (see page 98)

sewing needle

fabric glue (optional)

seam ripper (optional)

Difficulty rating

Challenging

Completed size

29cm wide x 17cm high x 16cm deep
(11½in wide x 6¾in high x 6¼in deep)

Prepare the pieces

1 Using the templates on page 109, cut out two body sections from hessian and copy the markings. Cut out the tummy, snout, stripes, nose, ears and eyes from black, white and grey fleece as directed on the templates. Cut a strip 1.5 x 25cm (½ x 10in) from the grey fleece; this will be used to secure the edges of the face. Cut the remaining grey fleece into 1.5 x 5cm (½ x 2in) strips (see Proggy strip template on page 101).

Hook the pieces

2 To secure the edges of the hessian face section, use the long strip of grey fleece to create a running stitch around the folded edge using the technique shown on page 106.

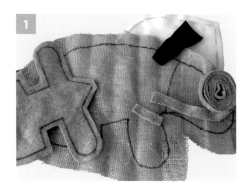

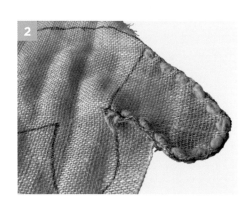

3 Secure the remaining edges of the hessian body sections with strips of grey fleece and using the technique shown on page 103. Fill in the outline, then trim any excess hessian using scissors. Fill in the body sections, but not the face, using the technique shown on page 102.

Join the body sections

4 Hold the body sections with the wrong sides together. Oversew from the tail to the neck (marked A–B on the template). Fold the front legs in half lengthwise towards the back of the badger, then oversew to make feet. Leave the front section open.

5 Position the tummy section against the base of the body, tucking the seam allowance shown on the template inside the body. Oversew in place.

Make the face

6 Position the black fleece stripes on the white fleece snout as shown in the photograph. Stab stitch along each edge to hold in place (see page 106).

7 Fold the snout in half, with the wrong sides together, and backstich around the outside edges, leaving the seam allowance shown on the template, to create a pocket. Turn the snout right side out and slip it over the hessian face section to check the fit and adjust as necessary. When you are happy with the fit, position the snout on the body and oversew in position.

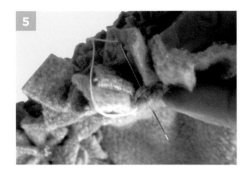

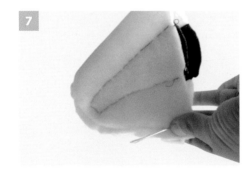

Add the ears

8 Position the ears at the top of the snout and about 1.5cm (½in) apart. Make one hole in the snout for each ear using the tip of a pair of scissors or a seam ripper. Push the two strips at the base of the ears through the holes in the snout and the hessian, and secure using the technique shown on page 105. Secure with fabric glue if desired.

Add the eyes

9 Make a hole in the centre of the white fleece circles and position on the snout. Attach the circles to the snout, using the safety eyes and the technique shown on page 105.

Completing the badger

10 Position the nose at the tip of the snout and backstitch in place.

11 Stuff the body, then oversew to close the opening at the front legs. If necessary, use scissors to trim the fleece covering the badger body so it is a uniform length, being careful not to cut the ears.

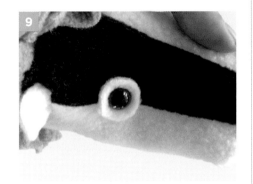

Try This!

A new coat

People traditionally used old grey coats to create proggy rugs. You can use this traditional fabric to give the badger's fur a rougher texture. You can also use the proggy technique for the striped face rather than sew it on.

Happy Hedgehog

This prickly pal would be welcome in any home. You will often find him snuffling among the autumn leaves in search of somewhere warm to sleep through the winter.

You will need

50 x 25cm (20 x 10in) hessian

50 x 50cm (20 x 18in) brown fleece

20 x 20cm (8 x 8in) beige fleece

one pair 12mm (½in) black safety eyes

250g (10oz) polyester soft toy stuffing

brown and beige sewing thread

fabric marker pen

scissors

ruler

pointed rag rug tool (see page 98)

sewing needle

fabric glue (optional)

Difficulty rating

Easy

Completed size

10cm high x 12cm wide x 17cm deep
(4in high x 4¾in wide x 7¾in deep)

Prepare the pieces

1 Using the templates on page 110, cut out the body sections and base from hessian and copy the markings. Cut out the face from beige fleece as directed on the template. Cut two strips 1.5 x 25cm (½ x 10in) from the beige fleece; this will be used to secure the edges of the hessian face and base. Cut the remaining brown fleece into 1.5 x 5cm (½ x 2in) strips with pointed ends (see Hedgehog strip template on page 101).

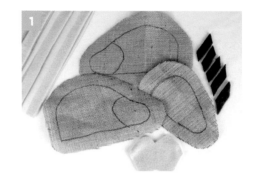

Hook the pieces

2 To secure the edges of the hessian face sections, use the long strips of beige fleece to create a running stitch around the folded edge using the technique shown on page 103.

3 Secure the edges of the hessian body sections using the technique shown on page 103, and strips of brown fleece. Once the outline is complete, trim any excess hessian using scissors.

4 Fill in the body sections using the technique shown on page 102.

Join the body sections

5 Hold the body sections with the wrong sides together. Starting at the nose and stitching towards the tail, oversew the sections together. Do not sew the base together. Red thread is used in the photograph to show the stitches.

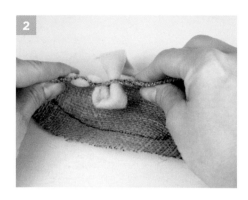

Make the face

6 Fold the face section in half with the wrong sides together and backstitch along the narrow end (marked A–B on the template), leaving the seam allowance shown on the template. Purple thread is used in the photograph to show the stitches.

7 Turn the face section right side out and use your fingers to smooth the seam flat.

8 Position the face over the hessian head section and oversew in place using small stitches.

9 Using the template markings as a guide, cut a small hole for one of the eyes in the face (do not cut the hessian beneath it). Attach one of the safety eyes using the technique shown on page 105. Repeat on the other side.

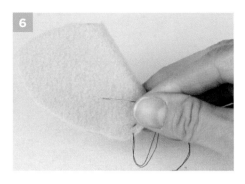

Completing the hedgehog

10 Position the base against the sides of the body with the wrong sides together. Starting at the nose and stitching towards the tail, oversew the sections together. Repeat on the other side, leaving a gap large enough to push the stuffing through.

11 Stuff the hedgehog, then oversew to close the opening.

Try This!

Make a mouse

To transform the hedgehog pattern into a mouse, you can use the same body shape. Fill each side panel with grey fleece, then add little round ears and a pink fleece tail.

Sassy Squirrel

Hiding away nuts for winter, his nose and bushy tail twitching busily among the trees, this fluffy friend also enjoys staying home with you when it is cold outside.

You will need

50 x 50cm (20 x 20in) hessian
75 x 50cm (30 x 20in) taupe fleece
25 x 25cm (10 x 10in) white fleece
5 x 5cm (2 x 2in) brown fleece
5 x 5cm (2 x 2in) beige fleece
one pair 12mm (½in) black safety eyes
250g (10oz) polyester soft toy stuffing
black sewing thread
fabric marker pen
scissors
ruler
pointed rag rug tool (see page 98)
sewing needle
fabric glue (optional)

Difficulty rating

Intermediate

Completed size

22cm high x 8cm wide x 24cm deep
(8½in high x 3in wide x 9½in deep)

Prepare the pieces

1 Using the templates on page 111, cut out the tail pieces from hessian and copy the markings. Cut out the body sections, head gusset, base and ears from taupe fleece. Cut the tummy from white fleece. Cut the remaining taupe fleece into 1.5 x 5cm (½ x 2in) strips (see Proggy strip template on page 101).

Hook the tail

2 Fold the hessian for one tail section along the marked lines and use the technique shown on page 103 to secure the fold with strips of taupe fabric. Fill in the outline until the folded edge is secure. Use scissors to trim any excess hessian. Repeat for the other hessian tail section.

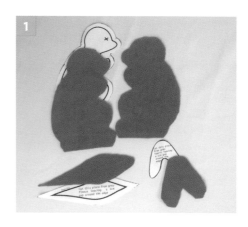

Make the body

3 Place the two body sections together with the right sides facing each other. Sew the sections together using a backstitch from the chin to the nose (marked A–B on the template), leaving the seam allowance shown on the template. Position the head gusset between the body sections and sew around one side, stopping where the ear will be positioned (marked B–C on the template).

4 Fold one ear in half lengthwise, then position it between the side and head gusset (marked C on the template). Make sure the open side of the ear faces towards the nose. Backstitch into position.

5 Repeat steps 1 and 2 to complete the other side of the head and ear. Sew down the back of the squirrel using a backstitch, stopping about 4cm (1½in) from the bottom (marked D–E on the template).

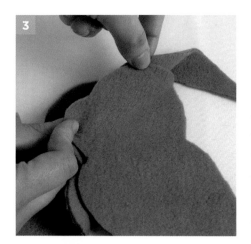

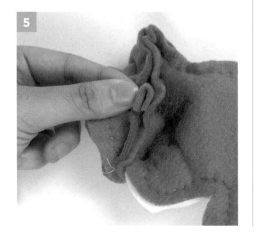

Add the tummy

6 Sew the darts where indicated on the white tummy section, using a backstitch (marked A and F on the template). Align the smaller dart at the top with the seam in the chin section, then sew down both sides using a backstitch to secure.

Add the eyes

7 Turn the body right side out. Position the eyes as marked on the template and attach them using the technique shown on page 105.

Add the base

8 Align the centre of the dart at the bottom of the tummy with the centre of the base section (marked F on the template). Oversew around each side from this point. Stuff the squirrel. Oversew the back closed.

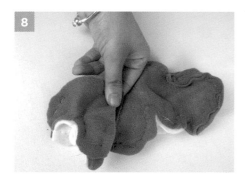

Add the tail

9 Hold the two tail sections with the wrong sides facing each other and oversew along the top edge and halfway along the bottom edge, leaving a gap large enough to push the stuffing through. Stuff the tail and oversew to close the opening. Stitch the tail in place on the body. If necessary, use scissors to trim the fleece covering the tail so it is a uniform length.

Make the nut

10 Roll some scraps of fleece into a ball and tie with thread to secure. Cover with a piece of beige fleece and stitch to create texture (using the photograph on page 23 as a reference). Cut a circle from brown fleece and add to the bottom to create the base of the nut. Stitch the nut in position between the paws.

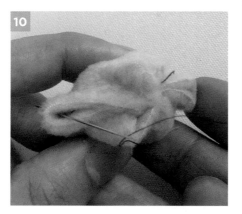

Try This!

Red squirrel

Change things up by making a red squirrel. These creatures have longer ears than their grey cousins, so elongate the pattern before you cut the pieces out. The colours of their coats vary with the seasons – from red in the summer to deep brown in the winter – just choose the shade of fleece you prefer.

Farmyard
Favourites

The farmer makes sure lamb and pig spend plenty of time in the fields. The duck likes to swim in the farm pond and preen himself at the water's edge. In the evenings, the bat flies out of the barn to eat insects.

Little Lamb

This bouncy spring lamb spends happy days playing with his friends, bleating happily as they frolic in the sun before taking shelter in the barn.

You will need

50 x 25cm (20 x 10in) hessian

50 x 50cm (20 x 20in) white fleece

50 x 25cm (20 x 10in) black fleece

5 x 10cm (2 x 4in) brown fleece

one pair 12mm (½in) black safety eyes

250g (10oz) polyester soft toy stuffing

black and white sewing thread

fabric marker pen

scissors

ruler

pointed rag rug tool (see page 98)

sewing needle

fabric glue (optional)

Difficulty rating

Easy

Completed size

14cm high x 19cm wide x 14cm deep
(5½in high x 7½in wide x 5½in deep)

Prepare the pieces

1 Using the templates on page 112, cut out the body sections from hessian and copy the markings. Cut out the legs and the top and sides of the head from black fleece as directed on the templates. Cut out the eyes from brown fleece. Cut a strip 1.5 x 25cm (½ x 10in) from the black fleece; this will be used to join the head to the body. Cut the white fleece into 1.5 x 5cm (½ x 2in) strips (see Proggy strip template on page 101).

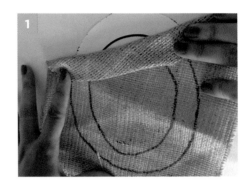

Hook the pieces

2 Secure the edges of the hessian body sections with strips of white fleece using the technique shown on page 103. Fill in the outline until the edges are secure. Once complete, trim excess hessian using scissors.

3 Fill in the body sections, using white fleece and the technique shown on page 102.

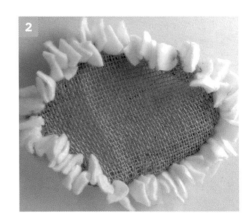

Make the legs

4 Fold one of the leg sections in half lengthwise with the wrong sides together, then backstitch along two sides (marked A–B on the template), leaving the seam allowance shown on the template. Do not stitch the strips that will attach the leg to the body. Turn right side out, then stuff the leg. Repeat with the remaining leg sections.

5 Push the four strips at the base of one of the legs through one side of the body at the point shown on the template, keeping them three strands of hessian apart, then tie them together using the technique on page 105. Secure with fabric glue if desired. Repeat for the other legs.

Make the head

6 Fold the face section in half with the wrong sides together and backstitch around the chin (marked C–D on the template), leaving the seam allowance shown on the template.

7 Cut small holes in the centres of the brown fleece circles. Make small holes in the head for the eyes at the points marked on the template. Attach the fleece circles to the head using the safety eyes and the technique shown on page 105.

8 With the wrong sides facing, align the centre of the top of the head (marked E on the template) with the sides and backstitch together as far as the chin (marked D on the template), leaving a gap large enough to turn the head right side out. Fold in the ears so that they will stick out when the head is turned right side out.

9 Thread the long strip of black fleece through the two slits in the back of the head panel so that the ends protrude from the back. Turn the head right side out, stuff, and then oversew to close the opening.

Completing the lamb

10 Hold the body sections with the wrong sides together. Starting at the front legs and stitching towards the neck, oversew the sections together. Stop sewing when you get to the centre of the back.

11 Push the ends of the strips of fleece through the sides of the body as close to the sewn edge as possible. Tie the strips together using a double knot. Secure with fabric glue if desired.

12 Continue to oversew the body sections together, leaving a gap between the legs large enough to add the stuffing. Stuff the body, then oversew the opening closed. If necessary, use scissors to trim the fleece covering the body so it is a uniform length, being careful not to cut the ears.

Try This!

Fluffy fleece

Swap out the fleece for natural felting fibre or some sheep's wool to create a super fluffy lamb. You can also try the loop technique shown on page 104.

Pink Pig

You will usually find this ball of fun splashing in the mud, or with his nose in a mound of acorns and his curly tail wagging. But he will happily enjoy a cuddle too.

You will need

50 x 50cm (20 x 20in) hessian

50 x 100cm (20 x 40in) light pink fleece

20 x 2cm (8 x ¾in) strip of black fleece

one pair 12mm (½in) black safety eyes

one 15cm (6in) pipe cleaner

250g (10oz) polyester soft toy stuffing

pink sewing thread

fabric marker pen

scissors

ruler

fabric marker pen

pointed rag rug tool (see page 98)

sewing needle

fabric glue (optional)

Difficulty rating

Easy

Completed size

15cm high x 20cm wide x 9cm deep
(6in high x 8in wide x 3½in deep)

Prepare the pieces

1 Using the templates on page 113, cut out the pieces for the body and base from hessian, copying the markings. Cut out the ears, nose and tail from the pink fleece. Cut a 1.5 x 50cm (½ x 20in) strip from pink fleece; this will be used to secure the underside. Cut the remaining pink fleece into 1.5 x 5cm (½ x 2in) strips (see Proggy strip template on page 101). Cut a strip of black fleece measuring 1.5 x 12cm (½ x 4¾in) for the nostrils.

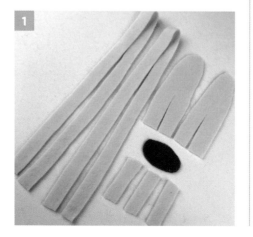

Hook the sections

2 Fold the hessian for one of the sides along the marked lines and use the technique shown on page 103 to work around the edge to secure the fold. Fill in the outline of the side in the same way. Continue until the folded edge is secure. Once the outline is complete, trim any excess hessian. Repeat the process for the other side.

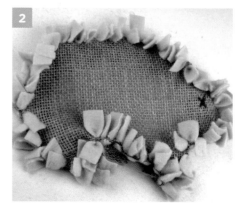

Add the eyes

3 Attach the eyes as marked on the template, using the technique on page 105. Fill in both sides of the pig with strips of pink fleece using the technique on page 102.

Making the base

4 Fold the hessian for the base panel along the marked lines. Use the 50cm (20in) strip of pink fleece to secure the edge, using the technique shown on page 103.

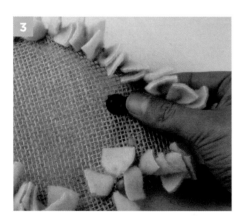

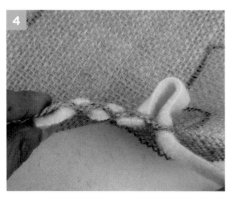

Add the ears and nose

5 Attach an ear to each side of the body by pushing the strips at the base of the ear through the hessian and tying the strips together, using the technique on page 105. Secure with a dab of fabric glue if desired. For clarity, the strips are shown in black in the photograph.

6 Hold the front and back body pieces with wrong sides together and oversew the two pieces together from the chin to the top of the snout (marked A–B on the template).

7 Cut slits in the nose as shown on the template. Cut the strip of black fleece in half and thread each piece in and out of one set of slits so you have four ends protruding from the back of the nose.

8 To attach the nose to the face, thread the black strips through the hessian, keeping them three strands of hessian apart. Tie the strips together on the wrong side using a double knot. Secure with a dab of fabric glue if desired.

Complete the pig

9 To attach the base panel, align the legs with the legs on the side panels and oversew around the edge of the base (marked B–C on the template).

10 Fold the tail in half lengthwise and sew along the long edge using a backstitch, leaving the seam allowance shown on the template. Turn the tail right side out and insert the pipe cleaner into the centre. Trim the end of the pipe cleaner so it is level with the end of the tail.

11 Sew together the back section of the sides (marked A–D on the template), leaving a gap large enough to push the stuffing through (marked D–C on the template). Add the tail by pushing the strips at the base through the hessian, three strands of hessian apart. Tie the strips together on the wrong side using a double knot. Secure the ends with fabric glue if desired.

12 Stuff the pig, then oversew the opening closed. Twist the tail around your finger to give it a curl. The pipe cleaner will help hold the tail's shape. If necessary, use scissors to trim the fleece covering the pig so it is a uniform length.

Try This!

Time for tea

Bring a splash of colour to the table with a pig-shaped tea cosy. Scale up the pattern to one-and-a-half or two times the size (see page 100) and omit the base. For added insulation, line the cosy with a layer of fleece.

Spooky Bat

Often out after midnight, especially on Halloween, this flappy black bat enjoys a spooky flight in the crisp night air in the farmyard before coming home to roost.

You will need

25 x 50cm (10 x 20in) hessian

50 x 75cm (20 x 30in) black fleece

5 x 5cm (2 x 2in) brown fleece

four 15cm (6in) pipe cleaners

one pair 12mm (½in) black safety eyes

250g (10oz) polyester soft toy stuffing

black sewing thread

fabric marker pen

scissors

ruler

pointed rag rug tool (see page 98)

sewing needle

fabric glue (optional)

Difficulty rating

intermediate

Completed size

13cm high x 30cm wide x 16cm deep
(5¼in high x 12in wide x 6¼in deep)

Prepare the pieces

1 Using the templates on page 114, cut out the body sections from hessian and copy the markings. Cut out the wings, ears and head from black fleece as directed on the templates. Cut eyes from brown fleece. Cut the remaining black fleece into 1.5 x 5cm (½ x 2in) strips (see Proggy strip template on page 101).

Hook the pieces

2 Secure the edges of the hessian body sections with strips of black fleece, using the technique shown on page 103. Fill in the outline until the folded edge is secure. Once the outline is complete, trim any excess hessian using scissors.

3 Fill in the body sections using the technique shown on page 102.

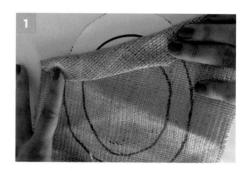

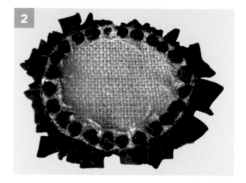

Making the wings

4 Bend one pipe cleaner in half along the edge of one wing as shown in the photograph. Fold the fabric over the pipe cleaner to enclose it and use a running stitch to hold it in place. The fabric should be wrapped around the pipe cleaner as tightly as possible. Repeat for the other wing.

5 Bend a pipe cleaner into a V shape and position it in the centre of one of the wings as shown in the photograph. Attach to the wing using the same technique as described in step 4. Repeat for the other wing.

6 Cut lengthwise along the centre of the tab on each wing as shown in the photograph to create two strips approximately 5cm (2in) long.

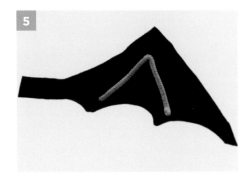

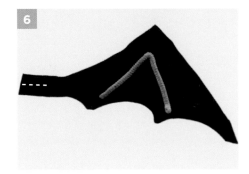

Completing the body

7 Push the two strips at the base of one of the wings through the centre of one body section, keeping them three strands of hessian apart. Tie the strips together using a double knot. Secure with fabric glue if desired. Repeat for the other wing on the other side of the body.

8 Hold the body sections with the wrong sides facing. Oversew the sections together, leaving a gap large enough to attach the face. Pink thread is used in the photograph to show the stitches.

Making the head

9 Fold the fleece head section in half lengthwise, and backstitch along the curved and long straight edge to create a pocket. Turn the face right side out.

10 Cut a hole in the centres of the brown fleece circles. Position the head over the opening in the body. Position a brown circle on the head and attach it using one of the safety eyes and the technique shown on page 105. This will attach the head to the body. Repeat on the other side of the face. Stuff the body, then oversew the opening closed. Stuff the head if desired.

11 Position the ears on each side of the head and oversew in place. If necessary, use scissors to trim the fleece covering for the body so it is a uniform length.

Try This!

Halloween visitor

Use strips of black plastic bags in place of the fleece to create a super spooky Halloween decoration.

Fluffy Duck

Quacking excitedly as she paddles her flappy feet among the reeds and pond weed, this fluffy duck will waddle back home to stay with you.

You will need

50 x 50cm (20 x 20in) hessian

100 x 50cm (40 x 20in) yellow fleece

25 x 20cm (10 x 8in) orange fleece

one pair 12mm (½in) black safety eyes

250g (10oz) polyester soft toy stuffing

yellow and orange sewing thread

fabric marker pen

scissors

ruler

pointed rag rug tool (see page 98)

sewing needle

fabric glue (optional)

Difficulty rating

Intermediate

Completed size

19cm high x 12cm wide x 11cm deep
(7½in high x 4¾in wide x 4¼in deep)

Prepare the pieces

1 Using the templates on page 115, cut out the body, wing and tummy sections from hessian and copy the markings. Cut out the bill and feet from orange fleece as directed on the templates. Cut a strip 1.5 x 25cm (½ x 10in) from the yellow fleece; this will be used to secure the wings. Cut the remaining yellow fleece into 1.5 x 5cm (½ x 2in) strips (see Proggy strip template on page 101).

Hook the pieces

2 Secure the edges of the hessian body sections with strips of yellow fleece, using the technique shown on page 103. Fill in the outline using strips of fleece as shown on the templates. Continue until the folded edge is secure. Once the outline is complete, trim any excess hessian using scissors. Repeat with the tummy and wing sections.

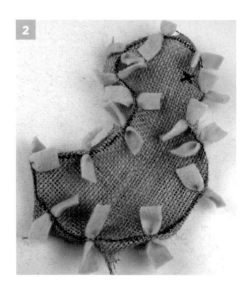

Add the eyes

3 Position one of the eyes on one of the body sections as marked on the template, and attach it using the technique shown on page 105. Repeat on the other side.

4 Fill in the hessian sections using strips of yellow fleece and the technique shown on page 102.

Add the feet

5 Push the four strips at the base of the feet through the tummy at the point shown on the template, keeping them three strands of hessian apart. Tie the strips together using a double knot. Secure with fabric glue if desired.

Add the wings

6 To attach the wings, cut the long strip of yellow fleece in half (black fleece is used in the photographs). Fold one strip in half and push both ends through the tip of one of the wings as shown on the template, then push each end through the body at the point shown on the template.

7 Pull the strip of fabric through the body then tie the strips together using the technique on page 105, adding fabric glue if desired. Repeat for the other wing.

Adding the tummy

8 Hold one of the body sections and the tummy section with the wrong sides together. Starting at the base and stitching towards the head (marked A–B on the template), oversew the sections together. Black thread is used in the photograph to show the stitches. Repeat for the other side.

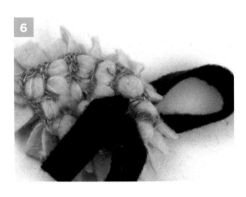

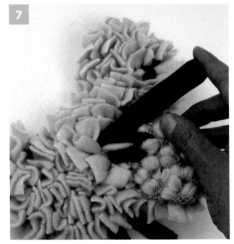

Making the bill

9 Hold the two bill sections with wrong sides facing and backstitch together along three sides (marked E–F on the template), leaving a 5mm (¼in) seam allowance. Do not stitch the strips that will attach the bill to the body. Black thread is used in the photograph to show the stitches. Turn right side out.

Completing the duck

10 Starting at the point where the tummy joins the sides, and stitching towards the head (marked B–C on the template), oversew the side sections together until you reach the point where you need to add the bill.

11 Push the eight strips at the base of the bill through the head at the point shown on the template, keeping them three strands of hessian apart. Tie the strips together in pairs using a double knot. Secure with fabric glue if desired.

12 Oversew the remaining seam (marked A–C on the template), leaving a gap large enough to push the stuffing through. Stuff the duck, then oversew the opening closed. If necessary, use scissors to trim the fleece covering the body so it is a uniform length, being careful not to cut the bill or feet.

Try This!

Feature feathers

Vary the colour of the fleece to create different breeds of ducks or alternatively to add splashes of colour or a feathery texture to the wings.

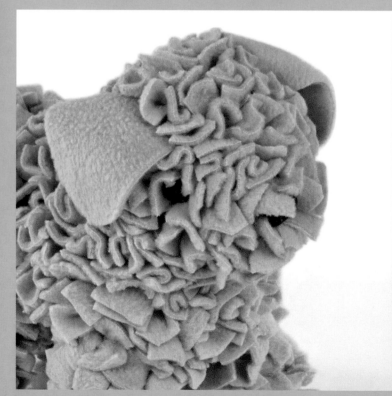

Perfect
Pets

If you are looking for a faithful friend,
then a kitten or puppy is likely to
be your pet of choice. The tortoise
appreciates a quiet home and
hibernates all winter. Meanwhile,
bunny enjoys being in the garden
and nibbling on carrots.

Cuddly Kitten

This cute ball of fluff likes nothing more than a game with a ball of string, or a scurrying mouse, before nuzzling in for a catnap on your lap.

You will need

50 x 50cm (20 x 20in) hessian

50 x 100cm (20 x 40in) black fleece

25 x 50cm (10 x 20in) white fleece

10 x 10cm (4 x 4in) pink fleece

one pair 12mm (½in) black safety eyes

60cm (24in) clear nylon fishing wire

250g (10oz) polyester soft toy stuffing

black sewing thread

fabric marker pen

scissors

ruler

pointed rag rug tool (see page 98)

sewing needle

fabric glue (optional)

Difficulty rating

Challenging

Completed size

24cm high x 13cm wide x 29cm deep
(9⅛in high x 5in wide x 11½in deep)

Preparing the pieces

1 Cut out the sides, front, feet and tail from hessian, using the templates on page 116, and copy the markings. Cut out the ears from black fleece. Cut a strip 1.5 x 25cm (½ x 10in) of black fleece; this will be used to attach the legs. Cut the remaining black fleece and the white fleece into 1.5 x 5cm (½ x 2in) strips (see Proggy strip template on page 101).

2 Secure the edges of the hessian shapes using the technique shown on page 103. Fill in the outlines using the colours instructed on the templates.

3 Fold the tail in half lengthwise and oversew along the long side (marked A–B on the template). Pink thread is used in the photograph to show the stitches.

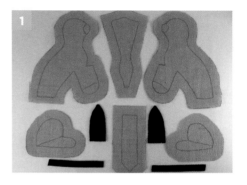

Assembling the body

4 For one of the front feet, fold the foot section up and around one front leg (marked C–D on the template) and oversew in place. Repeat with the other foot.

5 Position the front of the body against the sides with wrong sides together. Oversew from the base to the neck (marked E–F on the template). When you reach the front leg, sew the open side of the hessian so that there will be no open seams when you stuff the kitten. Repeat on the other side.

Adding the features

6 Add the eyes where they are marked on the template and secure using the technique on page 105. To make the whiskers, cut the nylon wire into four equal lengths. Using two lengths of wire on each side of the nose, thread them in and out of the hessian and secure them using double knots.

7 Create the head by sewing the side panels together where they join the front to just past the white section of the nose (marked F–G on the template).

8 Cut out the nose from pink fleece. Secure it to the face using a few small stab stitches.

Adding the ears

9 To add the ears, push the four strips of fabric at the base of one ear through the hessian on one side of the head, keeping them three strands of hessian apart. Tie them together in pairs using the technique on page 105. Secure with fabric glue if desired. Repeat on the other side of the head.

Adding the feet

10 Add the feet to the back legs by cutting the 1.5 x 25cm (½ x 10in) strip of black fleece in half (shown in yellow in the photograph). Thread one piece through the centre of one of the feet where it is marked on the template. The ends of the strip should be pushed through, keeping them three strands of hessian apart. Repeat for the other side.

11 Push the ends of the strip through the side panel where it is marked on the template. Make sure the two ends of the strip are three strands of hessian apart and secure them with a double knot. Repeat for the other side.

Completing the kitten

12 Sew together the two sides from the head to the base (marked G-H on the template), adding the tail as you go (marked A-A on the template). Stuff your cat, then oversew the base to close the opening (marked E-H on the template). If necessary, use scissors to trim the fleece covering the cat so it is a uniform length.

Try This!

Fluffy kitten

To make a truly furry kitten, use a natural felting fibre or wool rather than fleece to make the fur. The result will be a super fluffy finish. You may also want to try the loop stitch shown on page 104.

Darling Puppy

With floppy ears and a wagging tail, big eyes,
a happy smile, every puppy is adorable. And
this little fellow will not chew your slippers.

You will need

50 x 50cm (20 x 20in) hessian

50 x 100cm (20 x 40in) beige fleece

one pair 12mm (½in) black safety eyes

one 12mm (½in) black safety nose

250g (10oz) polyester soft toy stuffing

beige sewing thread

fabric marker pen

scissors

ruler

pointed rag rug tool (see page 98)

sewing needle

fabric glue (optional)

Difficulty rating

Intermediate

Completed size

18cm high x 23cm wide x 12cm deep
(7in high x 9in wide x 5in deep)

Prepare the pieces

1 Cut out the body, tummy and chin
from hessian, using the templates
on page 117, and copy the markings.
Cut out the ears and tail from the
beige fleece. Cut the remaining
fleece into 1.5 x 5cm (½ x 2in)
strips (see Proggy strip template
on page 101).

2 Secure the edges of the hessian
body sections using the technique
shown on page 103. Fill in the
outline of the body, followed by
the tummy and chin sections. Trim
any excess hessian using scissors.

Add the eyes

3 Secure the eyes in the positions
shown on the templates, using
the technique shown on page 105.
Fill in all the sections using the
technique shown on page 102.

Start to assemble the body

4 Line up one side of the body with the muzzle, then oversew together using a needle and beige thread (marked A–B on the template). Pink thread is used in the photographs to show the stitches. Repeat the process for the other side section.

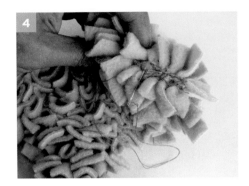

Complete the head

5 Push the four strips at the base of one of the ears through the hessian on one side of the head, about three strands of hessian apart, then tie them together using the technique on page 105. Secure with a dab of fabric glue if desired. Repeat on the second side.

6 Use a sewing needle and beige thread to sew together the front of the head, by oversewing from the point where the central head and two side panels join to the chin (marked A–C on the template). Push the nose through a gap in the stitching and secure in the same way as the eyes.

Complete the body

7 Align the legs on the tummy section with the legs on one of the side panels and oversew the sections together, starting at the chin and ending at the tail (marked C–D on the template).

8 Repeat for the other side of the tummy section. If the legs splay when you stand the dog up, remove a few pieces of fleece from the centre of the tummy.

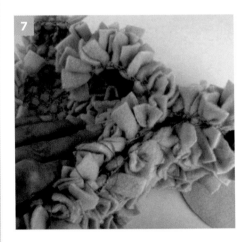

Add the tail

9 Fold the tail in half with right sides facing and use a backstitch to sew from the tip to the point where the strips begin (marked F–G on the template), leaving the seam allowance shown on the template. Turn right side out.

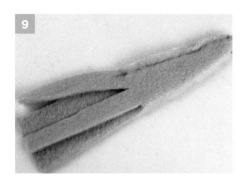

10 Oversew the side and tummy panels together to join the tummy of the back (marked D–E on the template), leaving a gap large enough to push the stuffing through (marked B–E on the template). Add the tail by pushing the strips at the base through the hessian, making sure the seam runs down the centre of the tail and the strips are three strands of hessian apart. Tie them together using the technique on page 105, and secure with a dab of fabric glue if desired.

Finish your puppy

11 Stuff the puppy and oversew the remaining open seams closed. If necessary, use scissors to trim the fleece covering the puppy so it is a uniform length, being careful not to cut the ears or the tail.

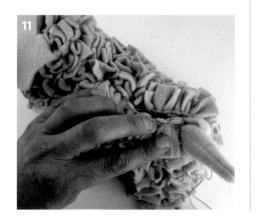

Try This!

Proggy portrait

Create a proggy version of your own pup by choosing fabrics that match his coat and adding stripes or patches as necessary.

Floppy Bunny

This bunny's big ears are listening for the farmer; his eyes are alert and his nose is twitching. He will mischievously nibble the crops and then hop home with his white tail bobbing.

You will need

50 x 50cm (20 x 20in) hessian

50 x 100cm (20 x 40in) white fleece

15 x 15cm (6 x 6in) pink fleece

one pair 12mm (½in) black safety eyes

250g (10oz) polyester soft toy stuffing

white sewing thread

fabric marker pen

scissors

ruler

pointed rag rug tool (see page 98)

sewing needle

fabric glue (optional)

Difficulty rating

Intermediate

Completed size

20cm high x 13cm wide x 10cm deep
(8in high x 5in wide x 4in deep)

Prepare the pieces

1 Using the templates on page 118, cut out the sides and tummy from hessian, copying the markings. Cut out the tail, nose and ears from the white and pink fleece as directed. Cut the remaining white fleece into 1.5 x 5cm (½ x 2in) strips (see Proggy strip template on page 101).

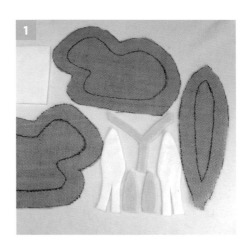

Hook the edges

2 Fold the hessian for one of the sides along the drawing line on the template and use the technique shown on page 103 to secure the fold. Continue until the folded edge is secure. Once the outline is complete, trim any excess hessian using scissors. Repeat the process for the second side and the tummy.

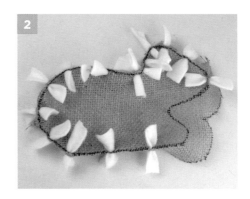

Add the eyes

3 Insert the safety eyes in the positions marked on the template using the technique shown on page 105.

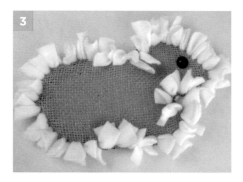

Assemble the tail

4 Place a ball of stuffing in the centre of the tail section. Fold two corners over the stuffing diagonally to make a tube and stitch the corners together. Repeat with the second pair of corners.

5 Continue to bring the edges of the fabric together and secure with stitches until you have a round tail. Secure the thread, but do not cut it, as you will use it to sew the tail to the body.

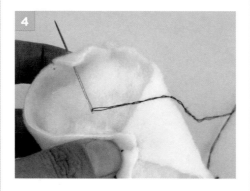

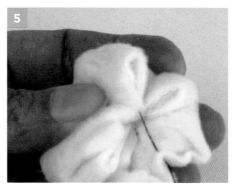

Assemble the ears

6 Use white thread to sew the pink inner ears to the centres of the larger white ears using stab stitch. If you do not want to sew them, you can attach them with a dab of fabric glue.

7 Push the strips at the base of one ear through the body panel as marked on the template. Position the strips about three strands of hessian apart and tie them together, using the technique on page 105. Add a dab of fabric glue to secure if desired. Repeat for the other ear.

Complete the body

8 Fill in the rest of the panels using the technique shown on page 102.

9 Position the tummy against the side pieces with right sides facing out and oversew together from the feet to the tail (marked A–B on the template) along both sides.

10 Sew from where the tummy joins the sides to the top of the head. Stop at the top of the head (marked A–C on the template) so that there is space to add the nose.

Add the nose

11 Push the strips at the end of the Y-shaped nose piece into the hessian using the same technique as for the ears. When you are happy with the position, tie the strips together on the inside to secure using double knots.

12 Oversew the body from the head to the tail, leaving a gap large enough to push the stuffing through (marked B–C on the template). Stuff the rabbit, then sew up the gap. Stitch the tail into position. If necessary, use scissors to trim the fleece so it is a uniform length.

Try This!

Poseable ears

To make the rabbit's ears more expressive, cut out two white shapes for each ear and sew them together before inserting a pipe cleaner into each one (like the pig's tail on page 35). Then you can position the ears in a floppy pose.

Tiny Tortoise

Slow and steady wins the race they say. This little guy has the life of Riley lounging in the summer sunshine and sleeping through the winter in his pretty patterned shell.

You will need

25 x 50cm (10 x 20in) hessian

50 x 40cm (20 x 15in) bright green fleece

50 x 40cm (20 x 15in) dark green fleece

one pair 12mm (½in) black safety eyes

250g (10oz) polyester soft toy stuffing

green sewing thread

scissors

ruler

pointed rag rug tool (see page 98)

sewing needle

seam ripper (optional)

Difficulty rating

Intermediate

Completed size

8cm high x 20cm wide x 12cm deep
(3in high x 8in wide x 5in deep)

Prepare the pieces

1 Using the templates on page 119, cut out the shell and base sections from hessian and copy the markings. Cut out the legs and head from dark green fleece as directed on the templates. Cut a strip 1.5 x 25cm (½ x 10in) from the dark green fleece; this will be used to secure the edges of the base of the shell. Cut the remaining dark green and bright green fleece into 1.5 x 5cm (½ x 2in) strips (see Proggy strip template on page 101).

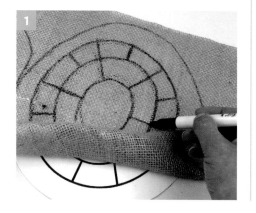

Make the legs

2 With right sides facing, use a backstitch to sew one of the leg sections together, leaving the seam allowance shown on the template. Do not sew together the strips as you will need to use them to attach the leg to the body. Turn the leg right side out and stuff. Repeat with the remaining leg pieces.

Make the head

3 With right sides facing, use a backstitch to sew the two head sections together along the curved edges, leaving the seam allowance shown on the template. Yellow thread is used in the photographs to show the stitches.

4 Decide where you want to place the eyes and make small holes with scissors or a seam ripper. Attach one of the safety eyes using the technique shown on page 105. Repeat on the other side. Turn the head right side out and stuff.

Make the shell base

5 To secure the edges of the hessian shell base section, use the long strip of dark green fleece to create a running stitch around the folded edge using the technique shown on page 103. Once the outline is complete, trim any excess hessian using scissors.

6 Decide on the placement of the legs around the base. Push the strips from the base of one leg through one side of the shell base, keeping the strips three strands of hessian apart. Tie the strips together using the technique on page 105. Secure with fabric glue if desired. Repeat for the other legs.

Make the shell

7 Secure the edges of the hessian shell section with strips of dark green fleece using the technique shown on page 103. Fill in the outline using strips of bright green fleece as shown on the templates. Once the outline is complete, trim any excess hessian using scissors. Fill the lines on the shell with dark green fleece and the spaces between them with bright green fleece using the technique shown on page 102 to complete the shell.

Complete the turtle

8 Use tacking stitches to attach the head to one end of the shell.

9 Hold the shell sections with the wrong sides facing and oversew together, leaving a gap large enough to push the stuffing through. Sew through the ends of the legs, but take care not to catch the fabric covering the shell in the stitches.

10 Stuff the shell, then oversew the opening closed. If necessary, use scissors to trim the fleece covering the shell so it is a uniform length.

Try This!

Shell effects

Working the shell in faux leather will give your tortoise shell a great texture. Another fantastic alternative is using a printed fleece, which will produce some interesting patterns on the shell.

Feathered
Friends

The plumage of these birds recalls
their diverse homes. The parrot's
bright feathers could only belong
in a tropical country, while the baby
penguin's grey covering is perfect
for an icy destination. The colouring
of the robin and owl help camouflage
them in woods and fields.

Pretty Parrot

This tropical bird loves to talk. His colourful plumage and fluffy feathers mean he looks equally at home perched on a pirate's shoulder or brightening up your house.

You will need

50 x 50cm (20 x 20in) hessian

25 x 25cm (10 x 10in) blue fleece

25 x 20cm (10 x 8in) yellow fleece

25 x 20cm (10 x 8in) white fleece

25 x 20cm (10 x 8in) black fleece

one pair 12mm (½in) black safety eyes

250g (10oz) polyester soft toy stuffing

white, blue, yellow sewing thread

fabric marker pen

scissors

ruler

pointed rag rug tool (see page 98)

sewing needle

fabric glue (optional)

Difficulty rating

Challenging

Completed size

38cm high x 10cm wide x 13cm deep
(15in high x 4in wide x 5in deep)

Prepare the pieces

1 Cut out the body and wings from hessian using the templates on page 120 and copy the markings. Cut out the eyes, tail and beak from the black, white, blue and yellow fleece as indicated on the templates. Cut a strip 1.5 x 25cm (½ x 10in) from the blue fleece; this will be used to attach the wings. Cut the remaining blue and yellow fleece into 1.5 x 5cm (½ x 2in) strips (see Proggy strip template on page 101).

Assemble the face

2 Use the tip of a pair of scissors to make a hole for the eye in each of the white face sections. Position the face sections onto the hessian body sections and attach using small running stitches with white thread. Attach the safety eyes to the face sections, inserting them through the holes and using the technique shown on page 105.

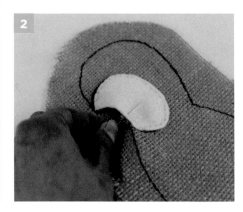

Hook the edges

3 Fold the hessian for one of the body sections along the drawing line on the template and use the technique shown on page 103 to secure the fold with strips of blue fleece. Repeat for the second body section and the wings using blue and yellow fleece as indicated on the templates. Fill in all pieces using the technique shown on page 102.

Make the tail and beak

4 Layer the three tail sections so that the longest piece is at the bottom and the shortest is at the top. Use blue thread and a needle to tack the three layers together 5mm (¼in) from the straight edge.

5 Arrange the beak sections as shown in the photograph. Sew them together using a backstitch and a 5mm (¼in) seam allowance in the order below, bending the black diamond to fit the contours of the white pieces, and create the shape of the beak. Using the lettering on the templates, sew together A–B, B–C, A–D, C–D, A–E and C–F.

6 When all four beak sections are attached to the central section, sew the two white sections together using a backstitch and leaving the seam allowance shown on the template, then sew the black sections together. Turn the beak right side out.

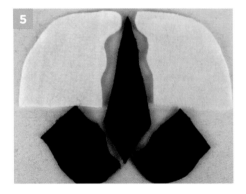

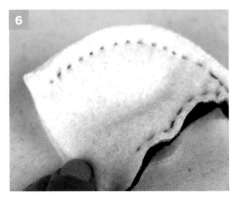

Attach the wings

7 Cut the long strip of blue fleece in half (yellow fabric is used in the photograph for clarity). Fold one strip in half and push both ends through the tip of one of the wings as indicated on the template, then push each end through the body at the point marked on the template.

8 Pull the strip of fabric through the body and tie the ends together using the technique on page 105, adding a dab of fabric glue to secure if desired. Repeat for the other wing.

Complete the parrot

9 Oversew the beak to the body sections using white thread. Align the beak with the face and start sewing at the top of the beak where the two white sections meet, down to the centre of the black section.

10 Using blue thread, join the body sections in the same way, starting at the beak and oversewing over the top of the head and down the back of the body to the tail. Align the centre of the tail with the point where the two back sections meet; stitch in place leaving a gap large enough to push the stuffing through.

11 Stuff the parrot, then oversew the open seam from the tummy to the tail. If necessary, use scissors to trim the fleece covering the parrot so it is a uniform length.

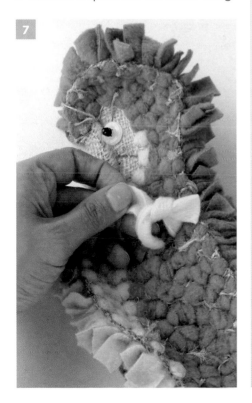

Try This!

Cotton feathers

This project works really well using scraps of cotton instead of fleece; it will fray slightly and give your parrot a more feathery look.

Wise Old Owl

This wise old owl is a real hoot! He certainly knows a thing or two about flying at night and sleeping all day – he would rather snooze with you.

You will need

50 x 50cm (20 x 20in) hessian

50 x 100cm (20 x 40in) leopard print fleece (any brown pattern will do)

25 x 25cm (10 x 10in) beige fleece

20 x 10cm (8 x 4in) yellow fleece

15 x 8cm (6 x 3in) white fleece

one pair 12mm (½in) black safety eyes

250g (10oz) polyester soft toy stuffing

black or brown sewing thread

fabric marker pen

pointed rag rug tool (see page 98)

sewing needle

fabric glue (optional)

Difficulty rating

Easy

Completed size

18cm high x 15cm wide x 9cm deep
(7in high x 6in wide x 3½in deep)

Prepare the pieces

1 Using the templates on page 121, cut out the body and wings from hessian, copying the markings.

2 Cut out the eyes and beak from the yellow fleece as directed. Cut out the inner eyes from the white fleece. Cut out the ears from the leopard print, along with a strip 1.5 x 25cm (½ x 10in) that will be used to attach the wings. Cut the remaining leopard print and beige fabric into 1.5 x 5cm (½ x 2in) strips (see Proggy strip template on page 101).

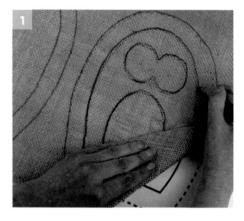

Hooking the edges

3 Fold the hessian for one of the sides along the drawing line on the template. Use the technique shown on page 103 to secure the folded edge.

4 Continue until the folded edge is secure. Once the outline is complete, trim any excess hessian using scissors. Repeat the process for the back and the wings.

Adding the features

5 To add the eyes, fold the white circles in half and then in half again. Snip a tiny piece from the centre point. Repeat with the yellow circles and align the holes. Alternatively, you may prefer to position the holes off-centre to change your owl's expression. Insert the safety eyes through the felt and hessian in the position marked on the template.

6 Secure the eyes using the technique shown on page 105, but do not make them too tight (just the first notch will be enough).

7 To add the beak, push each side of the yellow beak section through the hessian as indicated on the template. The two strips should be three strands of hessian apart. Tie the two sections in a double knot at the back. If desired, add a dab of fabric glue to secure the knot.

8 Attach the ears at the top of the head on the front using the same technique for attaching the beak. Insert in the positions marked on the template.

Finishing

9 Fill in the centres of the front, back and wings of the owl using the technique shown on page 102. Remember to fill in the tummy section with the beige and leave gaps around the eyes.

10 Join the front and back of the owl by oversewing the two sides together. For clarity, blue thread is used in the photograph.

11 To attach the wings, take half of the long leopard strip you kept to one side (for clarity, a grey strip is used in the photograph). Loop both ends through the wing, and then use the rag rug tool to push each end into the body, where it begins to widen after the head.

12 Pull the strip of fabric through the body, then tie the strips together using the technique on page 105, adding fabric glue if desired. Repeat for the other wing, then finish sewing up the side. Partially sew on the base, leaving a gap large enough to push the stuffing through. Stuff the owl, then oversew the open seam. If necessary, use scissors to trim the fleece covering the owl so it is a uniform length.

Try This!

Glove puppet

Leave off the base panel and do not stuff your owl to create a puppet. To create a snowy owl, use white fleece for the whole body.

Rockin' Robin

We may associate him with Christmas, but thanks to his natural curiosity, the little red-breasted friend will hop straight into your heart and stay there all year.

You will need

50 x 50cm (20 x 20in) hessian

75 x 50cm (30 x 20in) dark brown fleece

25 x 25cm (10 x 10in) red fleece

25 x 20cm (10 x 8in) white fleece

10 x 10cm (4 x 4in) yellow fleece

one pair 12mm (½in) black safety eyes

250g (10oz) polyester soft toy stuffing

black sewing thread

fabric marker pen

scissors

ruler

pointed rag rug tool (see page 98)

sewing needle

fabric glue (optional)

Difficulty rating

Intermediate

Completed size

18cm high x 15cm wide x 13cm deep
(7in high x 6in wide x 5in deep)

Prepare the pieces

1 Using the templates on page 122, cut out the body, chest and wing pieces from hessian, copying the markings. Cut out the beak from yellow fleece. Cut a 1.5 x 12cm (½ x 4¾in) strip of yellow fleece; this will be used to attach the beak. Cut two 1.5 x 12cm (½ x 4¾in) strips of brown fleece; these will be used to attach the wings. Cut the remaining brown, red and white fleece into 1.5 x 5cm (½ x 2in) strips (see Proggy strip template on page 101).

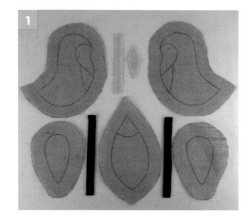

Hook the edges

2 Fold the hessian for one body section along the marked lines and use the technique shown on page 103 to work around the edge to secure the fold. Fill in the outline of the body section using dark brown fleece, red for the face, white for the chest. Continue until the folded edge is secure. Use scissors to trim any excess hessian. Repeat for the other pieces of hessian. Use dark brown fleece for the wings and red and white for the chest.

Add the eyes

3 Secure the safety eyes to the body sections in the positions marked on the template using the technique on page 105. Fill in all the hessian sections with strips of fleece following the colours shown on the templates, and using the technique on page 102.

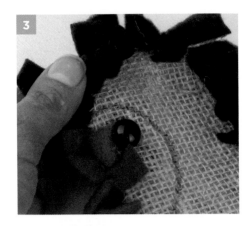

Add the wings

4 To attach the wings, fold one of the long brown strips in half and push both ends through the narrow tip of one of the wings. Yellow fleece is used in the photograph for clarity.

5 Push both ends through the body at the point where it begins to widen after the head, and about three strands of hessian apart. Pull the strip of fabric through the body, pull tight, then tie the strips together using the technique on page 105, adding a dab of fabric glue to secure if desired. Repeat for the other wing.

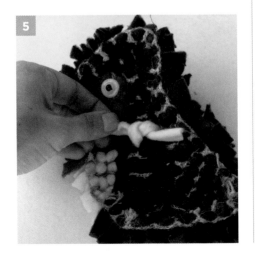

Add the chest and beak

6 Starting at the tail end of the body, oversew the chest panel into position along the line marked A–B on the template. Stop when you reach the head, then sew the other side from the tail to the head.

7 Cut along the two lines marked on the beak template and thread the strip of yellow fleece through them. Push the ends of the strip through the hessian using the technique on page 105. When you are happy with the position of the beak, secure in place in the same way as the wings.

Completing the robin

8 Oversew the sides together. A contrasting colour thread is used in the photograph to show the stitches. Hold the wrong sides of the pieces together and start at the point where the chest joins the sides, working to the top of the head (marked B–C on the template).

9 Sew the last section from the head to the tail, leaving a gap large enough to push the stuffing through (marked A–C on the template). Stuff the robin, then oversew the open seam. If necessary, use scissors to trim the fleece covering the robin so it is a uniform length.

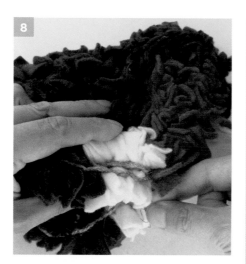

Try This!

Set of bowling pins

Create a set of bowling pins by making six robins and adding a weight, such as a bag of rice, inside the body of each one before sewing it up. Thanks to the stuffing, your bowling pins will land softly every time they are knocked over.

Baby Penguin

Although this adorable baby penguin enjoys waddling about in the ice and snow, he loves nothing better than to get out of the cold and stay inside where it is warm.

You will need

50 x 50cm (20 x 20in) hessian

75 x 50cm (30 x 20in) grey fleece

50 x 25cm (20 x 10in) black fleece

20 x 20cm (8 x 8in) white fleece

250g (10oz) polyester soft toy stuffing

grey sewing thread

fabric marker pen

scissors

ruler

pointed rag rug tool (see page 98)

sewing needle

fabric glue (optional)

Difficulty rating

Easy

Completed size

20cm high x 13cm wide x 10cm deep
(8in high x 5in wide x 4in deep)

Prepare the pieces

1 Using the templates on page 123, cut out the body, base and wings from the hessian, copying the markings. Cut a strip 1.5 x 12cm (½ x 4¾in) of black fleece for the eyes. Cut out the beak and feet from the black fleece. Cut a strip 1.5 x 25cm (½ x 10in) from the grey fleece; this will be used to attach the wings. Cut the remaining grey, black and white fleece into 1.5 x 5cm (½ x 2in) strips (see Proggy strip template on page 101).

Hook the body, wings and base

2 Fold the hessian for the front along the drawing line on the template and use the technique shown on page 103 to work around the edge to secure the fold. Fill in the outline of the body in grey and the outline of the head in black until the folded edge is secure. Once the outline is complete, trim any excess hessian using scissors. Repeat the outlining process for the back, wings and base.

Add the features

3 Using the eye positions marked from the template, push one end of the long black strip of fleece from the back through to the front of each eye and tie a double knot. Push the ends back through to the other side three strands of hessian from the first holes and tie them together using the technique on page 105. Add a dab of fabric glue to secure the knot if desired.

4 Add the beak in the same way as the eyes, pushing through the two strips at the base of the beak from the back to the front. The strips should be three strands of hessian apart. Tie the strips together at the back with a double knot to secure and add a dab of fabric glue to secure if desired.

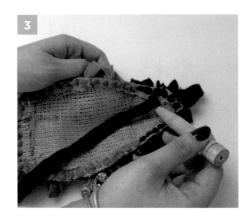

Add the feet and wings

5 Attach the feet at the base of the front, pushing the four strips of fleece through the hessian from front to back and tying the pairs together, using the technique on page 105. Add a dab of fabric glue to secure if desired.

6 Fill in the centres of the front, back, wings and base using the technique on page 102.

7 Place the front and back pieces together with wrong sides facing. Starting at the bottom, oversew the two pieces together. Stop about three-quarters of the way around so you can still get your hand inside the body.

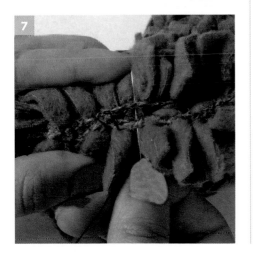

8 To attach the wings, cut the long strip of grey fabric in half (leopard print is used in the photograph). Fold one strip in half and push both ends through the tip of one of the wings as shown on the template, then push each end through the body at the point where it begins to widen after the head.

9 Pull the strip of fabric through the body and tie it together in a double knot as before. Secure with fabric glue if desired. Repeat for the other wing. Sew the rest of the front and back together. If you want to stuff your penguin, partially oversew the base to the body, leaving a gap large enough to push the stuffing through, then fill it with the stuffing. Oversew the opening closed. If necessary, use scissors to trim the fleece covering the penguin so it is a uniform length.

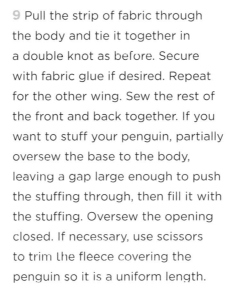

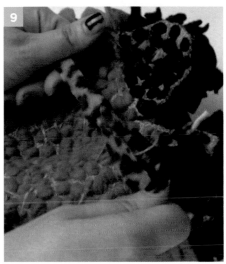

Try This!

Doorstop

Fill your penguin with rice or dried beans instead of polyester stuffing to make a friendly doorstop.

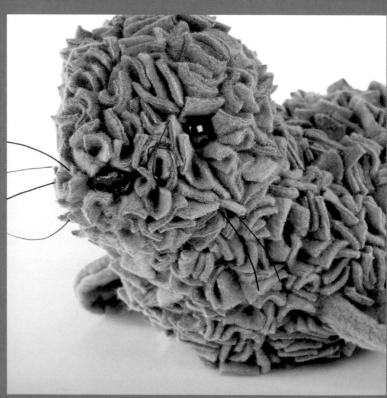

Water
Babies

Whether you are on the beach or
exploring a garden pond, there is
plenty of wildlife to be found. The
turtle and clown fish make their homes
in warmer waters, while the seal lives
in cooler climes. If you are lucky, you
may find a frog sitting on a lily pad.

Cute Clown Fish

The striped clown fish spends his days swimming around the coral reef and hiding in anemones, but he will gladly take the plunge and come live with you.

You will need

50 x 50cm (20 x 20in) hessian

50 x 50cm (20 x 20in) orange fleece

20 x 10 in. (50 x 25cm) white fleece

25 x 25cm (10 x 10in) black fleece

one pair 12mm (½in) black safety eyes

250g (10oz) polyester soft toy stuffing

black or white sewing thread

fabric marker pen

scissors

ruler

pointed rag rug tool (see page 98)

sewing needle

fabric glue (optional)

Difficulty rating

intermediate

Completed size

14cm high x 25cm wide x 10cm deep
(5½in high x 10in wide x 4in deep)

Prepare the pieces

1 Using the templates on page 124, cut out the body sections from hessian and copy the markings. Cut out the fins from orange fleece as directed on the templates. Cut the eyes from white fleece. Cut the remaining orange, white and black fleece into 1.5 x 5cm (½ x 2in) strips (see Proggy strip template on page 101).

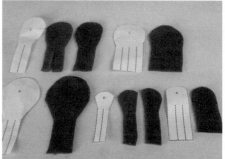

Hook the pieces

2 Secure the edges of the hessian body sections with strips of black fleece at the points where the orange and white sections join, using the technique shown on page 103. Fill in the outline using strips of orange and white fleece as shown on the templates. Continue until the folded edge is secure. Once the outline is complete, trim any excess hessian using scissors.

3 Fill in the black lines using the technique shown on page 102. Then fill in the orange and white sections of the body using the same technique. Do not fill in the face. Repeat for the other side.

Completing the face

4 Make a hole in the centre of one of the white fleece eyes. Position it on the face section and attach it using one of the safety eyes and the technique shown on page 105. Repeat on the other side. Fill in the face using strips of orange fleece.

Adding the fins

5 Push the two strips at the base of the side fins through one side of the body at the points marked D and E on the template, keeping them three strands of hessian apart. Tie the strips together using the technique on page 105. Secure with fabric glue if desired. Repeat on the other side.

6 Attach the two top fins and the tail fin to one side of the body at the points marked A, B and C on the template, positioning them close to the edge so that they will be in the centre of the body when the sides are sewn together.

Completing the fish

7 Hold the body sections with wrong sides facing and stripes aligned. Starting at the chin and stitching towards the tail, start to oversew the sections together.

8 When you reach the fin, hold it to one side and continue sewing until you have sewn past the tail, leaving a gap large enough to push the stuffing through.

9 Stuff the fish, then oversew the opening closed. If necessary, use scissors to trim the fleece covering the fish body so it is a uniform length, being careful not to cut the fins.

Try This!

Creating scales

For a scaly effect, round off the edges of the strips of fleece. You can increase the effect by using different materials for each of the stripes to create more texture.

Snuggly Seal

Twitching his whiskers and eager to play, diving for fish and flapping his flippers for fun, this friendly baby seal will swim and splash his way into your heart.

You will need

45 x 45cm (18 x 18in) hessian

100 x 45cm (40 x 18in) grey fleece

60cm (24in) black nylon fishing line

one pair 12mm (½in) black safety eyes

one 12mm (½in) black safety nose

250g (10oz) polyester soft toy stuffing

grey sewing thread

fabric marker pen

scissors

ruler

pointed rag rug tool (see page 98)

sewing needle

fabric glue (optional)

Difficulty rating

Intermediate

Completed size

15cm high x 25cm wide x 15cm deep
(6in high x 10in wide x 6in deep)

Prepare the pieces

1 Using the templates on page 125, cut out the body, tummy and back of the head sections from hessian and copy the markings. Cut out the flippers and tail from grey fleece as directed on the templates. Cut the remaining fleece into 1.5 x 5cm (½ x 2in) strips (see Proggy strip template on page 101).

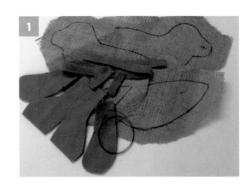

Hook the pieces

2 Secure the edges of the hessian body, tummy and head sections with grey fleece using the technique shown on page 103. Fill in the outline until the folded edge is secure. Once the outline is complete, trim any excess hessian using scissors.

3 Fill in the body, tummy and head sections using the technique shown on page 102.

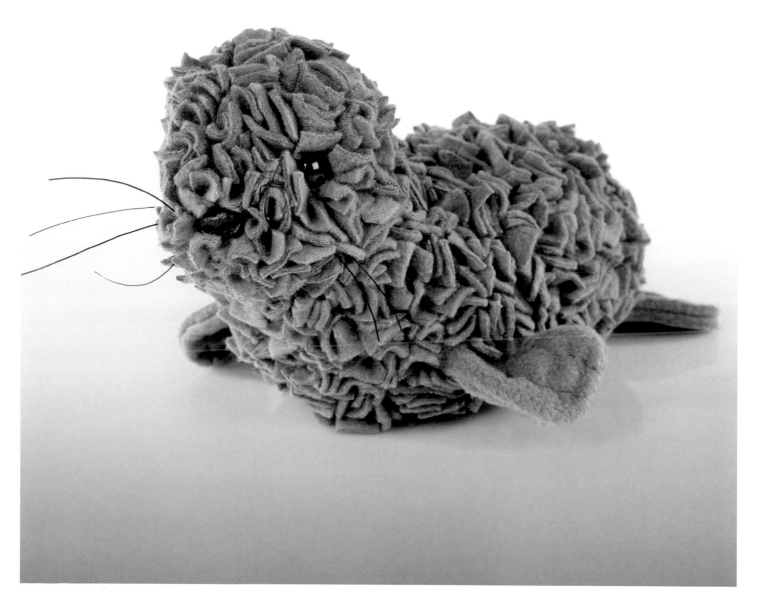

Make the flippers and tail

4 Hold two flipper sections with wrong sides facing and backstitch together, leaving the seam allowance shown on the template. Do not stitch the strips that will attach the flippers to the body. Repeat with the remaining flipper sections and the tail.

5 Turn the flippers and tail right side out and use a backstitch to mark the details on the flippers and tail. Cut into the fabric to make the joining strips as marked on the template.

6 Push the two strips at the base of the tail into the wider end of the tummy section at the point shown on the template, keeping them three strands of hessian apart. Tie the strips using the technique on page 105. Secure with fabric glue if desired.

7 Attach the flippers to the sides of the body as marked on the template in the same way.

Add the eyes and whiskers

8 Attach one of the safety eyes to one of the body sections as marked on the template, using the technique shown on page 105. Repeat on the other side.

9 Cut the black nylon fishing line into four equal lengths. Thread one length through the seal's nose. Repeat with the other lengths, then tie the wires together in pairs using a double knot.

Completing the seal

10 Hold the body sections with wrong sides facing. Starting at the back of the head and stitching towards the chin (marked A–B–C on the template), oversew the sections together. Leave a gap in the stitching at the nose to allow for the black plastic nose. Yellow thread is used in the photograph to show the stitches.

11 Attach the safety nose in the gap in the stitching using the technique shown on page 105.

12 Continue sewing the body sections together (marked C–D on the template) working towards the flipper. Position the tummy section and oversew along one side until you reach the tail (marked D–E on the template). Repeat on the other side. Oversew the remaining seam, from the head to the tail, leaving a gap large enough to push the stuffing through.

13 Stuff the seal, then oversew the opening closed. If necessary, use scissors to trim the fleece covering the body so it is a uniform length, being careful not to cut the whiskers, flippers and tail.

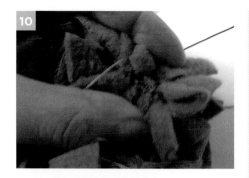

Try This!

Make a walrus

To make a walrus, use brown fleece to cover the body, rather than grey, and add a pair of impressive tusks made from white fleece.

Flappy Turtle

With a perfectly patterned shell, this sea-dwelling creature loves to swim, sunbathe and dive into tropical waters. He will joyfully paddle his way into your life.

You will need

25 x 45cm (10 x 18in) hessian

45 x 45cm (18 x 18in) bright green fleece

25 x 45cm (10 x 18in) taupe fleece

one pair 12mm (½in) black safety eyes

250g (10oz) polyester soft toy stuffing

green sewing thread

fabric marker pen

scissors

ruler

pointed rag rug tool (see page 98)

sewing needle

seam ripper (optional)

Difficulty rating

Intermediate

Completed size

7cm high x 28cm wide x 32cm deep
(2¾in high x 11in wide x 12½in deep)

Prepare the pieces

1 Using the templates on page 126, cut out the shell and base sections from hessian and copy the markings. Cut out the chin, flippers and head from bright green fleece as directed on the templates. Cut a strip 1.5 x 25cm (½ x 10in) from the taupe fleece; this will be used to secure the edges of the base of the shell. Cut the remaining bright green and taupe fleece into 1.5 x 5cm (½ x 2in) strips (see Proggy strip template on page 101).

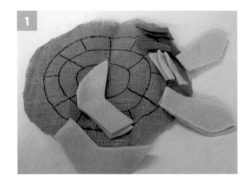

Make the flippers

2 With right sides facing, use a backstitch to sew two of the back flipper sections together, leaving the seam allowance shown on the template. Do not sew together the strips at the end of the flipper as you will use these to attach the flipper to the body. Turn the flipper section right side out. Repeat with the remaining back flipper pieces.

3 Join the front flipper sections using the same technique as above.

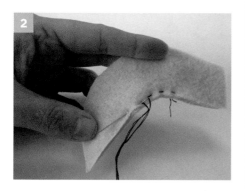

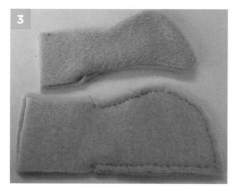

Make the head

4 Sew the head sections together from the nose to the neck (marked A–B on the template) using the same technique as the flippers. Insert the chin (marked A–C and A–D on the template), leaving a gap to push the stuffing through.

5 Make a small hole with a pair of scissors or seam ripper for each eye. Attach using the technique shown on page 105. Turn the head right side out and stuff.

Make the shell base

6 To secure the edges of the hessian shell base section, use the long strip of taupe fleece to create a running stitch around the folded edge using the technique shown on page 103.

7 Decide on the placement for the flippers. Push the strips from the end of one flipper through the shell base, making sure they point towards the tail end and are three strands of hessian apart. Tie the strips together using the technique on page 105. Secure with fabric glue if desired. Repeat for the other flippers.

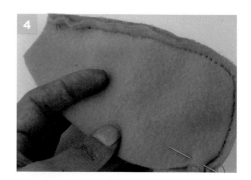

Make the shell

8 Secure the edges of the hessian shell section with strips of bright green fleece on the marked lines, using the technique shown on page 103. Fill in the outline using strips of taupe fleece as shown on the templates. Once the outline is complete, use scissors to trim any excess hessian.

9 To complete the shell, fill the lines on the shell with bright green fleece and fill the spaces between them with taupe fleece, using the technique shown on page 102.

Complete the turtle

10 Use tacking stitches to attach the head to the front end of the shell.

11 Hold the shell sections with the wrong sides facing and oversew them together, leaving a gap large enough to push the stuffing through. Sew through the ends of the flippers, but take care not to catch the fabric covering the shell.

12 Stuff the shell, then oversew the opening closed. If necessary, use scissors to trim the fleece covering so it is a uniform length.

Try This!

Cosy friend

The turtle's shell makes a great hot water bottle cover. Scale up the pattern so that the shell will hold your hot water bottle and leave an opening at the head or tail to slide the bottle in.

Crazy Frog

Happily hopping from lily pad to lily pad, this crazy frog makes croaky conversation with his froggy friends about all the adventures he'll have with you.

You will need

25 x 45cm (10 x 18in) hessian

45 x 45cm (18 x 18in) green fleece

25 x 25cm (10 x 10in) 12mm plastic mesh

1 pair 12mm (½in) black and green safety eyes

250g (10oz) polyester soft toy stuffing

green sewing thread

fabric marker pen

scissors

ruler

pointed rag rug tool (see page 98)

sewing needle

fabric glue (optional)

Difficulty rating

Challenging

Completed size

16cm high x 9cm wide x 16cm deep
(6¼in high x 3½in wide x 6¼in deep)

Prepare the pieces

1 Using the templates on page 127, cut out the body sections from hessian and copy the markings. Cut out the legs from plastic mesh as directed on the templates. Cut the feet from green fleece. Cut two strips 1.5 x 38cm (½ x 15in) from the green fleece; these will be used to secure the edges of the face sections. Cut the remaining green fleece into 1.5 x 5cm (½ x 2in) strips (see Proggy strip template on page 101).

2 To secure the edges of one of the hessian body sections, use the long strip of green fleece and work a running stitch around the folded edge, using the technique shown on page 103. This will be the base of the body.

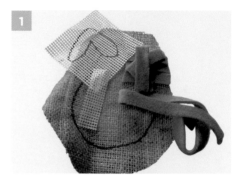

Hook the top of the frog's body

3 Secure the edges of the second hessian body section with strips of green fleece, using the technique shown on page 103. Fill in the outline until the folded edge is secure. Once the outline is complete, trim any excess hessian using scissors. Fill in this body section with strips of green fleece, using the technique shown on page 102. Use scissors to trim any excess hessian.

Make the legs

4 Cut the remaining strips of green fleece into quarters to make them small enough to push through the holes in the plastic mesh.

5 Use these small pieces of fleece to fill the leg sections, using the technique shown for hessian on page 102. Take care not to tear the mesh when using the tool. Fill every hole with a piece of fleece.

6 Push the two strips at the base of one of the feet through two holes in the mesh. Tie the strips together using the technique on page 105. Secure with fabric glue if desired. Repeat for the other feet.

7 Trim the excess mesh from the edges of the legs. Take care not to cut too close to the fleece strips or the mesh will not hold them in place.

8 Use scissors to trim the fleece covering the legs so that it is a uniform length, being careful not to cut the feet.

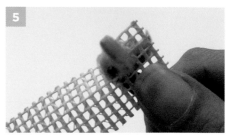

Completing the frog

9 Position the eyes on the head section of the body and attach using the technique shown on page 105.

10 Hold the body sections with the wrong sides facing. Oversew the head section from shoulder to shoulder. Pink thread is used in the photograph to show the stitches.

11 Continue to oversew the body sections together, adding the legs as you work by stitching through the body and the leg at the same time. Make sure you use three or four stitches for each leg so that they are securely attached. Stop when you have a gap just large enough to push the stuffing through.

12 Stuff the body, then oversew the opening closed. If necessary, use scissors to trim the fleece covering for the body so it is a uniform length, being careful not to cut the legs or feet.

Try This!

Recycled bags

Thin plastic is a fantastic alternative material to cover the frog's legs and body. Look for plastic shopping bags in greens and browns, or even mix in brighter colours to give your frog spots or stripes.

Tools

The proggy technique began as a way to recycle materials using everyday equipment, but there are some tools that will make it easier.

To push the strips of fabric through the hessian base you need a pointed instrument known as a proggy tool. Traditionally, these are made from turned wood, but if you cannot find one you can use a pencil or even a ballpoint pen that has run out of ink.

You can cut the fabric strips using a pair of scissors – a sharp pair will cut through the fabric faster than a blunt pair. You can also use a rotary cutter and cutting board (which are often used to cut fabric for quilting). The board provides a safe surface for the cutting tool, and the grid markings on it will make it easy to cut strips the same width. A dedicated strip cutter board is another useful tool that will make cutting strips easy.

To speed up the process even more, you can buy a special strip snip tool, which turns the long strips into shorter ones that are all the same length. To use it, wind a long fabric strip around the tool, and then cut through the central gap to create uniform lengths of fabric. Having pieces the same length will help reduce the need to trim your proggy animal when you have finished it.

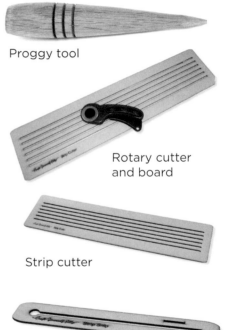

Proggy tool

Rotary cutter and board

Strip cutter

Strip snip

Assemble all the tools and materials you need before you begin.

Materials

The instructions for each animal include a list of the materials and equipment you will need. Make sure you have them before you begin.

Hessian

The strips of fabric for the fur or feathers are hooked onto hessian. Choose a medium-weight hessian – the weave of a lightweight hessian will be too loose to hold the fabric strips in place, and a heavyweight one will be too tight.

Fleece

Fleece is used to cover the hessian on all of the creatures in this book, but the proggy technique will work with almost any fabric. Fleece is soft and does not fray; it makes a minimal amount of mess while the strips are being cut and is lightweight, hypoallergenic and machine washable, which makes it easier to keep the creatures clean.

Felt

Felt is a great alternative to fleece as it creates a firmer texture but looks the same. It usually requires the same amount of material as fleece.

Cotton and T-shirt Fabrics

Strips of a woven cotton fabric will fray, so make the strips longer than recommended – 6 x 2cm (2½ x ¾in) is ideal. You will also need to insert the strips into the hessian so that they are closer together – two to three strands of hessian apart. This means you will need 50 to 100% more fabric than if you were using fleece, depending on the weight of the material.

Plastics

Recycled plastic shopping bags make a brilliant alternative to fleece. They are especially effective if you are making a water creature as it gives a shiny finish. You will need 50% more plastic than fleece.

Sheep's Fleece

Using wool from a sheep – especially if it has been washed but not spun – allows you to create some amazing effects for some of the animals with fluffier coats. You may need to tie it onto the hessian to secure it. You are likely to need twice as much wool than fleece fabric to get a dense finish.

Eyes and Noses

A lot of the animals have plastic safety eyes and noses. If correctly inserted, these are secure, making them ideal for children's toys. If you are sure that children will not play with your proggy creatures, you can use buttons instead. Another alternative is to hook through lengths of fabric to make the eyes and nose.

Enlarging and transferring templates

The templates in this book need to be enlarged on a photocopier, or by using a computer scanner and printer, before you can use them.

Each template needs to be enlarged by 200%. The sections are printed in different colours to make them easy to follow. There is no need to cut out the paper templates for the hessian sections – just place them under the fabric and you will be able to see the outline through the spaces between the threads. Use a fabric marker pen with a broad tip to trace the design onto the fabric. This makes the template much easier to follow – especially if this is your first proggy creation – and there's no need to worry about the marks showing on your finished creature as they will be hidden by the proggy covering.

Each hessian section has two marked lines: an inner, solid line that marks the area you will fill with fabric strips, and an outer, broken line that is the shape you follow when cutting out the fabric. Once you have cut out the fabric, the border around the solid outline is folded over and secured in place with proggy strips to prevent the hessian from fraying as you work. This means there is no need to tack or sew the edges before you begin. It also gives you a stable edge to sew along when you join the sections together, which makes assembling the animals much easier.

When you trace the templates onto the hessian, be sure to include any additional markings, for example the position of the eyes or wings and where different coloured sections fall, such as on the turtle shell or penguin. This will help you to finish your project as it is much harder to add in those marks once you have filled the sections with proggy strips.

Trace the outline through the hessian, making sure you include the markings for the coloured sections and any features.

Cut out the template shapes for the fleece sections as directed on the template.

Cut out the paper templates for the fleece elements of the animals, such as feet, ears and tails. Pin them onto the fleece, then cut them out. The template will state how many elements are required and which colour of fleece to cut them from.

For some sections, such as the body of the badger, you need to cut two shapes from the same template. The shapes need to be a mirror image of each other so you must flip the template over before marking and cutting the second shape.

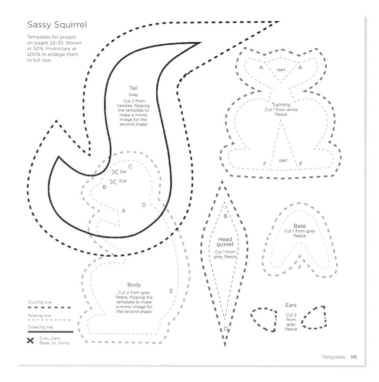

Sassy Squirrel

Templates for project on pages 22–25. Shown at 50%. Photocopy at 200% to enlarge them to full size.

Tail
Gray
Cut 2 from hessian, flipping the template to make a mirror image for the second shape

C Ear
B Eye
A
D

Body
Cut 2 from grey fleece, flipping the template to make a mirror image for the second shape

E

A dart A

Tummy
Cut 1 from white fleece

F dart F

B

Head gusset
Cut 1 from grey fleece

D

Base
Cut 1 from grey fleece

F

Ears
Cut 2 from grey fleece

Cutting line
Sewing line
Drawing line
Eyes, Ears, Beak, or Joints

Templates 111

The template sections are shown in different colours to help differentiate them.

Measuring and cutting the proggy Strips

Proggy strips were traditionally measured using the side of a matchbox, which created a rectangle measuring 5 x 1.5cm (2 x ½in). We use a template (see right) to measure them. This size is used for all the creatures in this book except the hedgehog, which has pointed strips (see bottom template on right). Proggy is a very forgiving technique, so you do not have to be super accurate about the length and width of your strips. However, the better you are

at keeping the size uniform, the less trimming you will need to do to your finished creature. To make cutting the strips quicker and easier, you can use a rotary cutter and board and a strip snip tool.

If you want to experiment by making creatures with long, shaggy coats, or try your hand at proggy rugs, you may want to make the strips longer than this. Or you can use a variety of lengths to create raised areas to add texture to your work. Alternatively, you can try the loop technique shown on page 106.

Proggy strip 1.5 x 5cm (½ x 2in)

Hedgehog strip 1.5 x 5cm (½ x 2in)

Techniques

The proggy technique – pushing strips of fabric into hessian – is a versatile one. Making the creatures also requires some hand sewing.

The basic proggy method

All the projects use the basic proggy stitch. It is incredibly simple and requires 5cm x 1.5cm (2 x ½in) strips of fabrics (see template on page 101). To make a stitch you must always work from the back (wrong side) of the hessian.

1 Use the proggy tool to make a hole in the hessian by inserting it between the threads to push them apart. Do not worry about making the hole too large – it will close up again when you make the next hole.

2 Use the proggy tool to push a strip of fabric about halfway through the hole, pushing it from the corner of one end rather than the centre. (It is harder to push the strip if you work from the centre.)

3 Use the proggy tool to make a second hole three or four strands of hessian away from the first. Do not be tempted to make the holes any closer than this or the hessian will begin to curl and you want it to stay flat.

4 Use the proggy tool to push the other end of the fabric strip through the second hole to the front of the hessian.

5 Adjust the ends of the strips as you go to keep your work even.

6 If you used fleece, or another fabric that will not fray, and your finished project has some stray strips or looks uneven, you can use a pair of scissors to trim the surface.

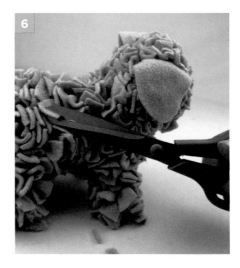

Securing the edges of the hessian

To prevent the edges of the hessian section from fraying, fold over the edges and work through both layers of fabric to secure them.

Fold the hessian along the lines marked on the template, and working around the edge, use the proggy technique to secure the edge. When you get to a curved section, 'pin' sections together with pieces of fabric, then join these to secure the whole edge. This helps to prevent the hessian from bunching at one end.

Use pieces of fabric to 'pin' the curved edges.

Fill in the sections between the 'pins' until the entire edge is secure.

Weaving

For some animals, you need to secure the edge of the hessian without using proggy strips. Do this using the weaving technique and long strips of 1.5cm (½in) wide fabric. To do this, always work from the back (wrong side) of the fabric.

1 Fold the edge of the hessian as marked on the template. Use the proggy tool to make a hole through both layers of fabric in the same way as for the basic proggy method (see opposite page).

2 Use the proggy tool to push one end of the strip of fabric through the hole. Pull it all the way through, from the back to the front, leaving a 2cm (¾in) tab at the back. Push the strip from the corner of one end rather than the centre. (It is harder to push the strip if you work from the centre.)

3 Use the proggy tool to make a second hole six to eight strands of hessian away from the first. As you become more experienced with the technique, you can place them closer together if you wish.

4 Use the proggy tool to push the other end of the fabric strip through the hessian, from the front to the back, and pull it all the way through to create a stitch. Do not pull too tightly or the fabric will bunch up.

5 Repeat steps 1 through 4, weaving the fabric in and out of the hessian to create a running stitch around the edge.

The weaving technique creates a running stitch around the folded edge of the hessian.

Loop stitch

As an alternative to the basic proggy method, you can use a loop stitch to make a curly coat for your animals. You will need long strips of fleece that are 1.5cm (½in) wide. This stitch is worked from the back to the front of the fabric.

1 Use the proggy tool to make a hole in the hessian by inserting it between the threads to push them apart. Do not worry about making the hole too large – they will close up again when you make the next hole.

2 Use the proggy tool to push one end of the strip of fabric through the hole, from the front to the back, so that about 2cm (¾in) is left in the front (right side). Push the strip from the corner of one end rather than the centre. (It is harder to push the strip if you work from the centre.)

3 Use the proggy tool to make a second hole three to four strands of hessian away from the first. Do not be tempted to make the holes any closer than this or the hessian will begin to curl.

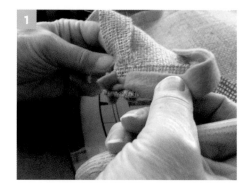

4 Fold over 1.5–2cm (½–¾in) of the fabric strip and use the proggy tool to push the folded end through the hessian to create a loop.

5 Repeat steps 3 and 4 to create a series of loops on the front (right side) of the hessian. Adjust the loops as you go to keep your work even.

6 When you get to the end of the strip of fabric, push the end through to the front of your work. It is important to keep the beginning ends of the strips at the front of your work as this prevents the loops from unravelling.

Inserting safety eyes and noses

Push the shaft of the eye or nose through the hessian from the front to the back in the position marked on the template. Push on the washer until it is secure.

Tying on limbs

For some of the animals, a long strip of fleece on the limb is used to attach the legs and other limbs. The point where these are attached to the body is usually marked on the template shapes.

1 At the point marked on the template (or the desired position), use the proggy tool to make a hole in the limb by inserting it between the hessian threads to push them apart. Push both ends of the long strip of fabric through the limb from the front through to the back and keeping them three strands of hessian apart. Push the strips through the body in the same way, from the front to the back.

2 Use a double knot to tie together the ends of the strip of fabric. If the creature is going to be given to a child as a toy, secure the knot with a dab of fabric glue.

Tying on feet and ears

Many of the creatures have feet and ears that are attached to the body using tabs cut into the fleece.

1 At the point marked on the template (or the desired position), use the proggy tool to make a hole by inserting it between the hessian threads to push them apart. Push one tab through the hessian from the front to the back. Repeat with a second tab three strands of hessian away from the first.

2 Use a double knot to tie the tabs together. If the creature is going to be given to a child as a toy, secure the knot with a dab of fabric glue.

Sewing and making up

Assembling most of the projects in this book requires a small amount of hand sewing, but you only need four simple stitches.

Oversewing

This stitch is used to join the hessian sections together. Align the sections to be joined (with the wrong sides together) and make a few small stitches in the edge of one of them to secure the thread. Insert the needle through the edge of both sections from one side to the other and pull the thread firmly through so that the stitch holds the edges together. Repeat, making the stitches 3–6mm (⅛–¼in) apart. Do not worry if you can see the stitches – they will be hidden by the proggy strips.

Backstitch

Some of the creatures have features that are sewn together, such as the flippers on the turtle and the puppy's tail. Hold the sections of fabric together, as directed in the instructions. Insert the needle from the front to the back of both pieces to make a stitch, then bring the needle back to the front to make a second stitch. Insert the needle into the second hole of the first stitch and back up to the front again about 5mm (¼in) further on to make a continuous line of stitching. Continue until the seam is finished.

Stab and running stitches

This small stitch is used to join two different colours of fabric, for example the ears on the bunny and the nose on the fox. Align the fabric pieces as directed in the instructions and pin them together. Working with the front side facing you, sew them together using a running stitch, which has small stitches on the right side and larger ones on the wrong side (where they will not be seen).

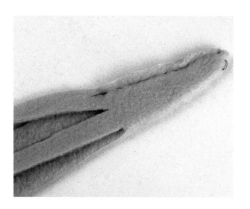

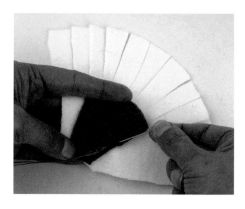

Proggy possibilities

The instructions for each of the creatures include a suggestion for something you can do to make your project a little different.

The alternative ideas include scaling templates up to make a bigger animal, as well as suggested uses for the finished items, such as hot water bottle cover, doorstop or tea cosy. The alternative adaptations for the projects often suggest different materials you can use to give your project a different texture.

The proggy technique can also be used to make fantastic home decorating projects, such as cushions, rugs and blankets. Cushions and rugs make ideal keepsakes when created using strips of fabric made from favourite clothes you and your family members no longer wear.

Cushions are one the easiest things to try as they are simple squares, although you can try more interesting shapes if you wish. You can make a proggy front for a cushion and sew on a fabric backing.

The proggy technique was traditionally used to make rugs, and these still make great statement pieces. Working on a proggy rug or blanket is a great way to get friends and family involved by asking each of them to add a few pieces to the design.

If you are making a large piece and want to incorporate a pattern or some writing in the design, draw a mirror image of it onto the back of the hessian so it appears correctly on the front.

If you want to have some fun, you can start to experiment with different materials, as almost any fabric, wool, or ribbon will work. The proggy technique is a great way to recycle old clothes or use up scraps from other projects. Just bear in mind that the materials you use to construct your animal will affect the way you clean it, but if your project will be decorative, then go wild!

Resources

UK
Craft Yourself Silly
www.craftyourselfsilly.com

Hobbycraft
www.hobbycraft.co.uk

Hochanda TV
www.hochanda.com

Amazon
www.amazon.co.uk

Etsy
www.etsy.com

and independent retailers

US
Pat Catan's
www.patcatans.com

Amazon
www.amazon.com

Etsy
www.etsy.com

Jo-Ann Stores Inc
www.joann.com

Friendly Fox

Templates for project on pages 10–13. Shown at 50%. Photocopy at 200% to enlarge them to full size.

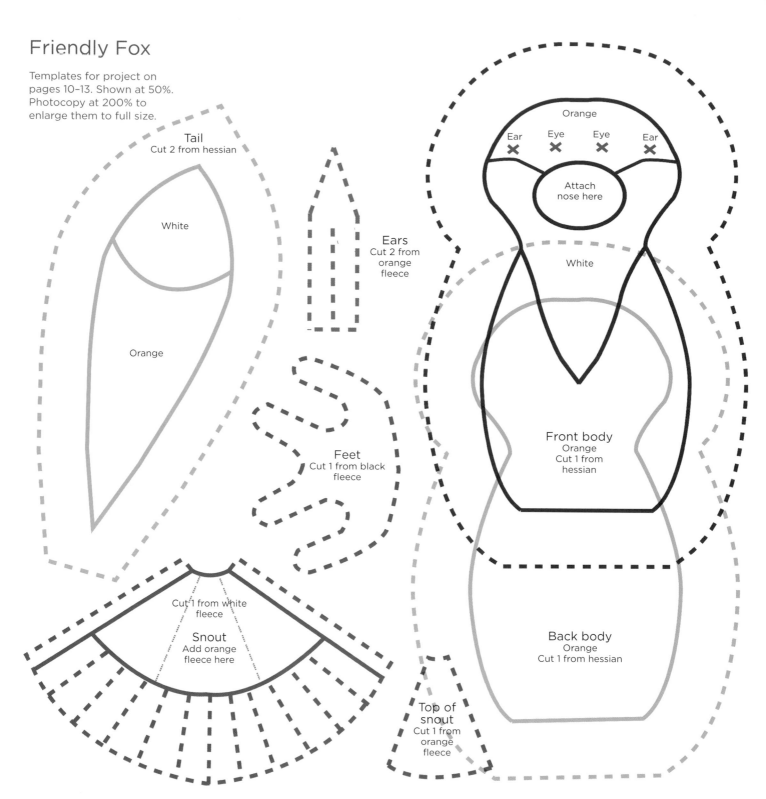

Tail
Cut 2 from hessian

White

Orange

Ears
Cut 2 from orange fleece

Feet
Cut 1 from black fleece

Cut 1 from white fleece
Snout
Add orange fleece here

Top of snout
Cut 1 from orange fleece

Orange

Ear   Eye   Eye   Ear

Attach nose here

White

Front body
Orange
Cut 1 from hessian

Back body
Orange
Cut 1 from hessian

Big Bold Badger

Templates for project on pages 14–17. Shown at 50%. Photocopy at 200% to enlarge them to full size.

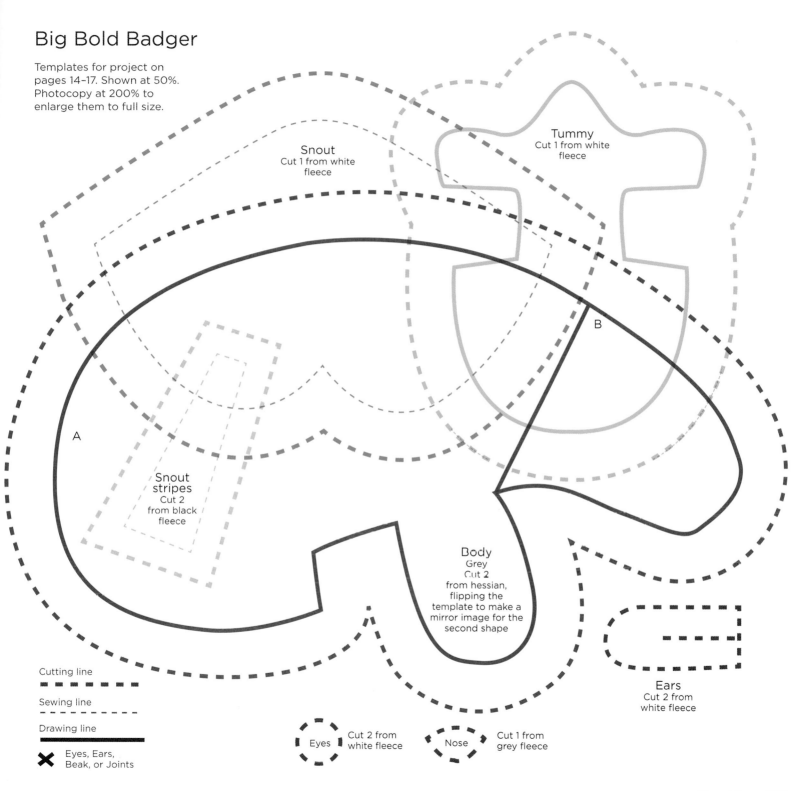

Snout
Cut 1 from white fleece

Tummy
Cut 1 from white fleece

B

A

Snout stripes
Cut 2 from black fleece

Body
Grey
Cut 2 from hessian, flipping the template to make a mirror image for the second shape

Cutting line
Sewing line
Drawing line
✗ Eyes, Ears, Beak, or Joints

Ears
Cut 2 from white fleece

Eyes Cut 2 from white fleece

Nose Cut 1 from grey fleece

Happy Hedgehog

Templates for project on pages 18–21. Shown at 50%. Photocopy at 200% to enlarge them to full size.

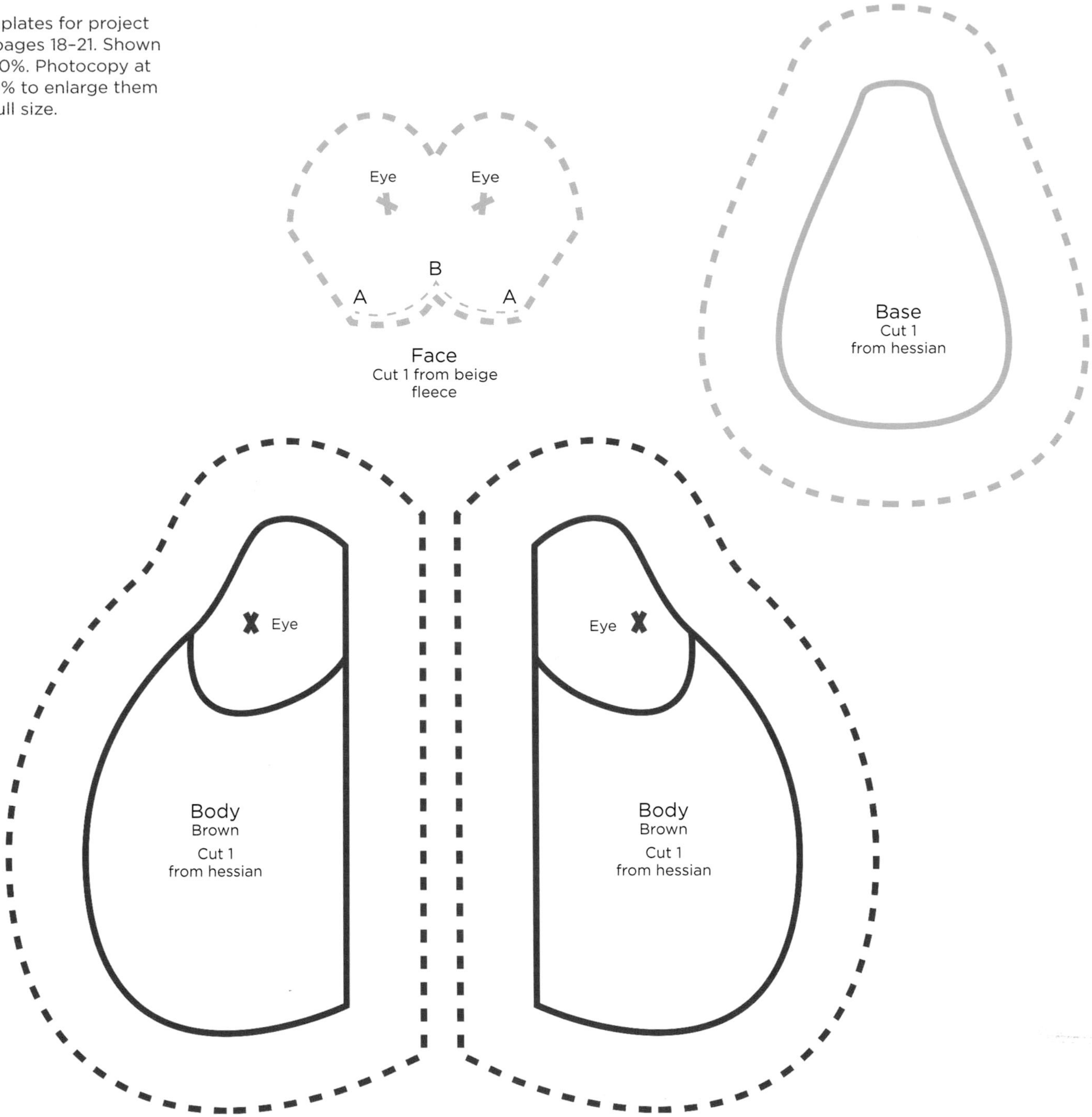

Eye

Eye

B

A

A

Face
Cut 1 from beige fleece

Base
Cut 1
from hessian

X Eye

Eye X

Body
Brown

Cut 1
from hessian

Body
Brown

Cut 1
from hessian

Sassy Squirrel

Templates for project on pages 22–25. Shown at 50%. Photocopy at 200% to enlarge them to full size.

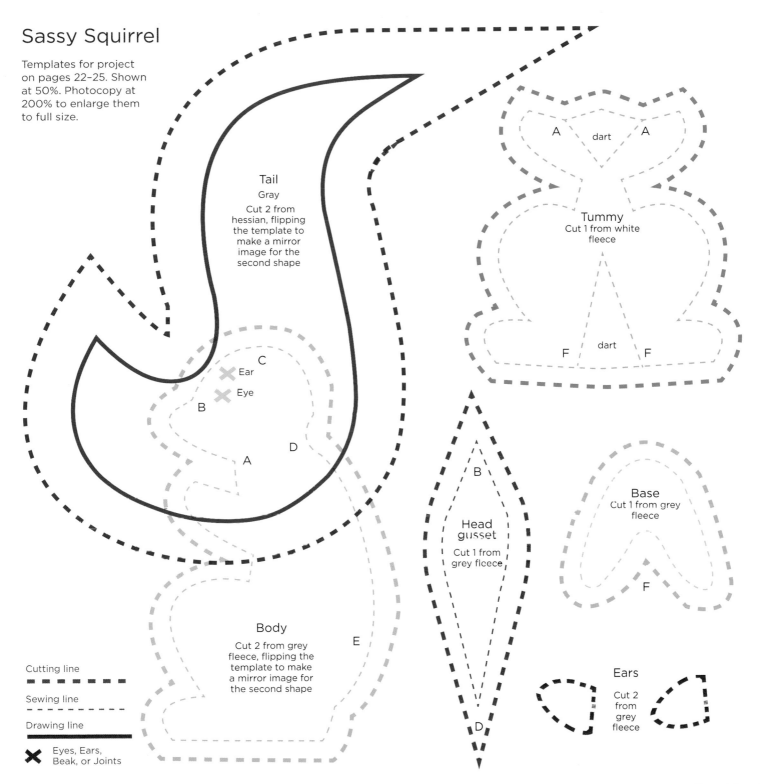

Tail
Gray
Cut 2 from hessian, flipping the template to make a mirror image for the second shape

A — dart — A

Tummy
Cut 1 from white fleece

F — dart — F

C
✕ Ear
✕ Eye
B
D
A

Body
Cut 2 from grey fleece, flipping the template to make a mirror image for the second shape

E

B
Head gusset
Cut 1 from grey fleece

D

Base
Cut 1 from grey fleece

F

Ears
Cut 2 from grey fleece

Cutting line

Sewing line

Drawing line

✕ Eyes, Ears, Beak, or Joints

Little Lamb

Templates for project on pages 28–31. Shown at 50%. Photocopy at 200% to enlarge them to full size.

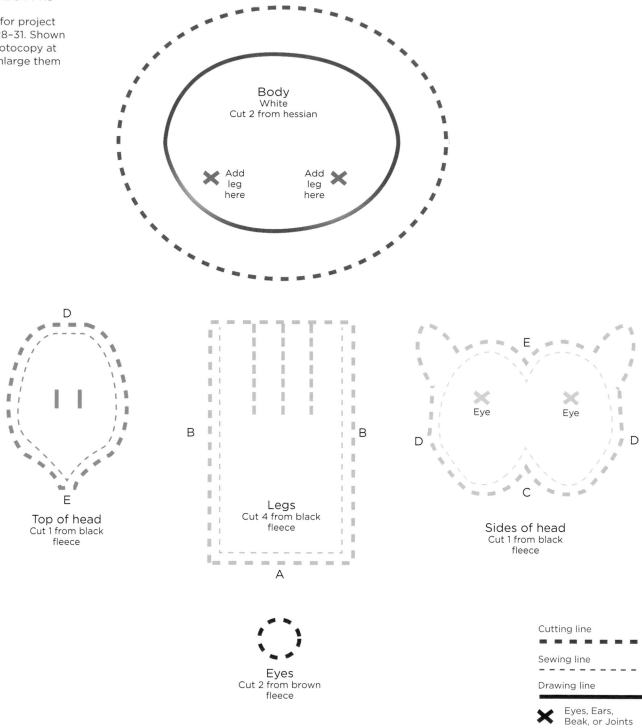

Body
White
Cut 2 from hessian

✖ Add leg here   Add leg here ✖

D

E

Top of head
Cut 1 from black fleece

B   B

A

Legs
Cut 4 from black fleece

E

D   D

C

Sides of head
Cut 1 from black fleece

Eye   Eye

Eyes
Cut 2 from brown fleece

Cutting line
– – – – – –

Sewing line
- - - - - -

Drawing line
———

✖ Eyes, Ears, Beak, or Joints

Pink Pig

Templates for project on pages 32–35. Shown at 50%. Photocopy at 200% to enlarge them to full size.

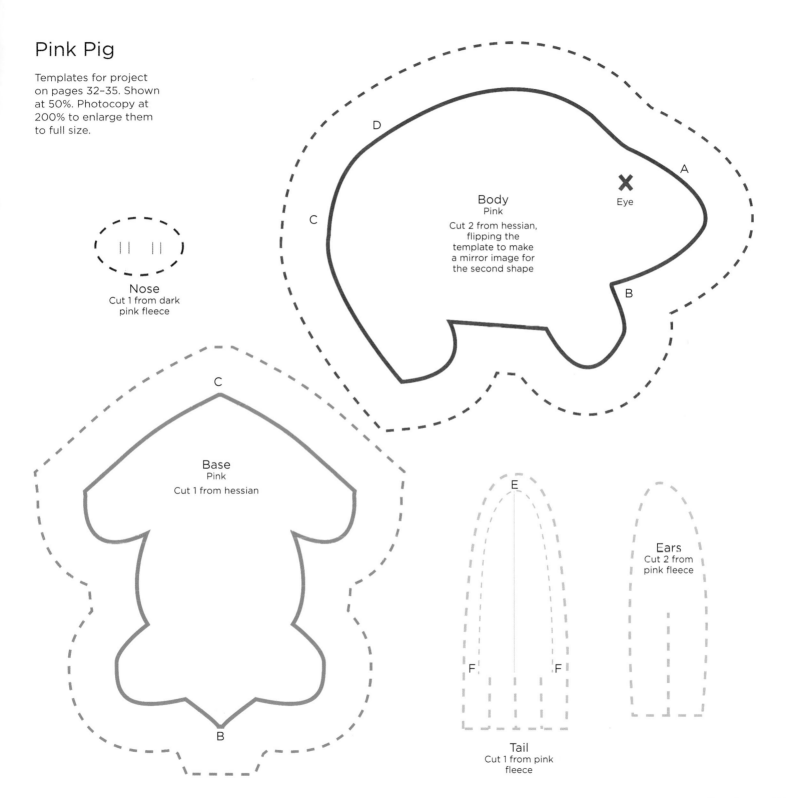

Nose
Cut 1 from dark pink fleece

Body
Pink
Cut 2 from hessian, flipping the template to make a mirror image for the second shape

Eye

A

B

C

D

Base
Pink
Cut 1 from hessian

C

B

Tail
Cut 1 from pink fleece

E

F   F

Ears
Cut 2 from pink fleece

Spooky Bat

Templates for project on pages 36–39. Shown at 50%. Photocopy at 200% to enlarge them to full size.

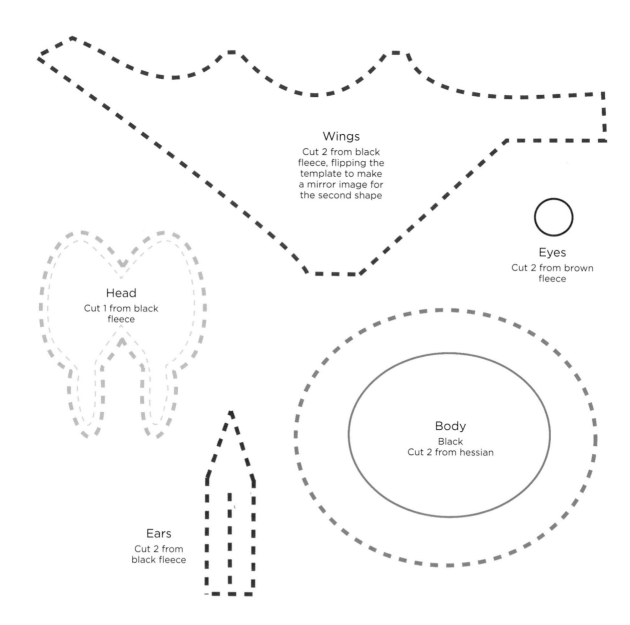

Wings
Cut 2 from black fleece, flipping the template to make a mirror image for the second shape

Eyes
Cut 2 from brown fleece

Head
Cut 1 from black fleece

Ears
Cut 2 from black fleece

Body
Black
Cut 2 from hessian

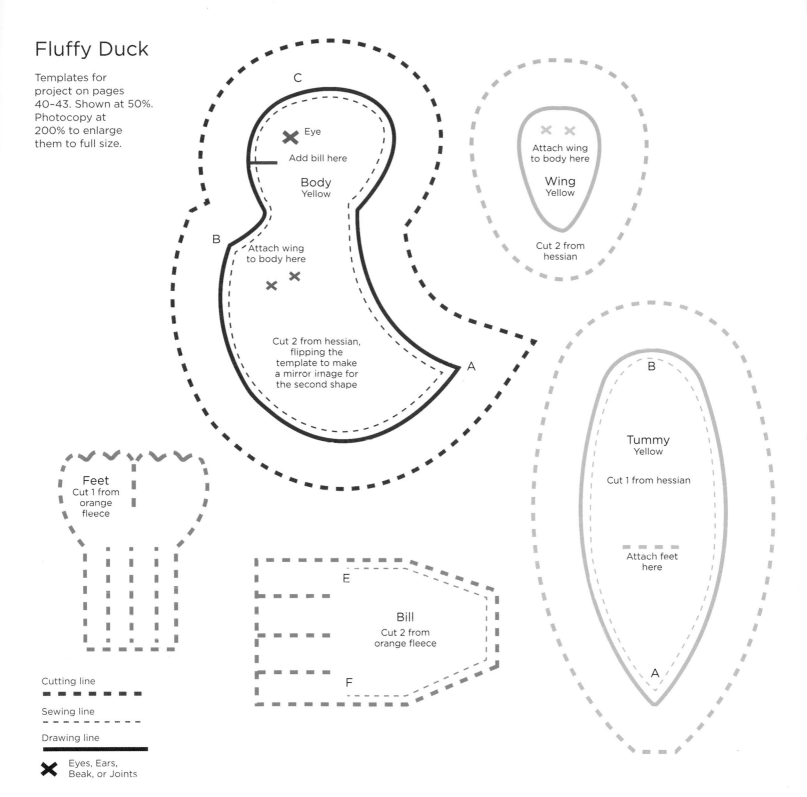

Fluffy Duck

Templates for project on pages 40–43. Shown at 50%. Photocopy at 200% to enlarge them to full size.

C

Eye

Add bill here

Body
Yellow

B

Attach wing to body here

Cut 2 from hessian, flipping the template to make a mirror image for the second shape

A

Wing
Yellow

Attach wing to body here

Cut 2 from hessian

Feet
Cut 1 from orange fleece

Bill
Cut 2 from orange fleece

E

F

B

Tummy
Yellow

Cut 1 from hessian

Attach feet here

A

Cutting line

Sewing line

Drawing line

Eyes, Ears, Beak, or Joints

Cuddly Kitten

Templates for project on pages 46–49. Shown at 50%. Photocopy at 200% to enlarge them to full size.

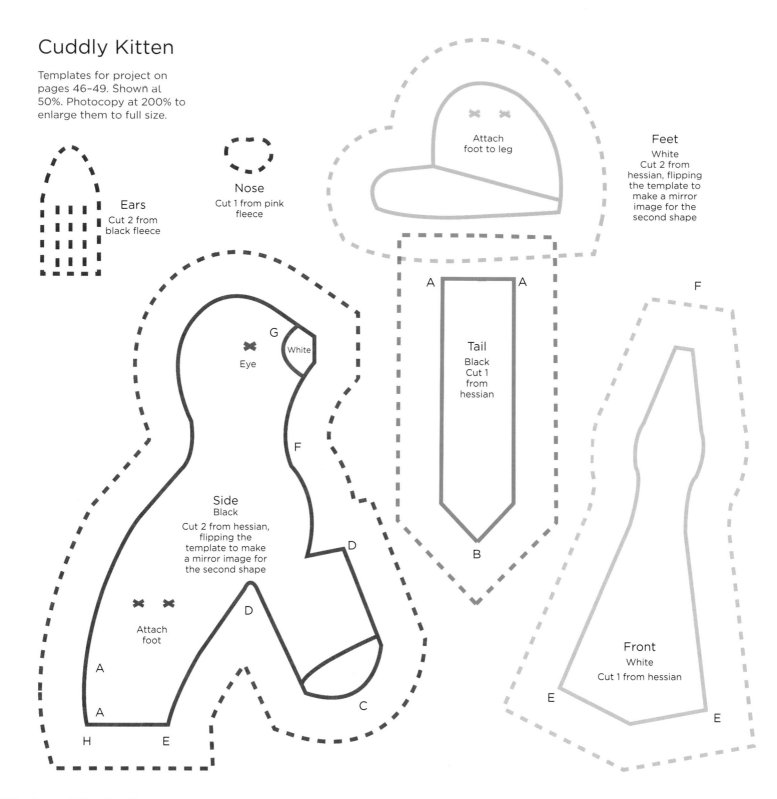

Ears
Cut 2 from black fleece

Nose
Cut 1 from pink fleece

Attach foot to leg

Feet
White
Cut 2 from hessian, flipping the template to make a mirror image for the second shape

Tail
Black
Cut 1 from hessian

A · A

B

Side
Black

Cut 2 from hessian, flipping the template to make a mirror image for the second shape

Eye

White

G

F

D

D

C

Attach foot

A

A

H · E

Front
White
Cut 1 from hessian

F

E

E

Darling Puppy

Templates for project on pages 50–53. Shown at 50%. Photocopy at 200% to enlarge them to full size.

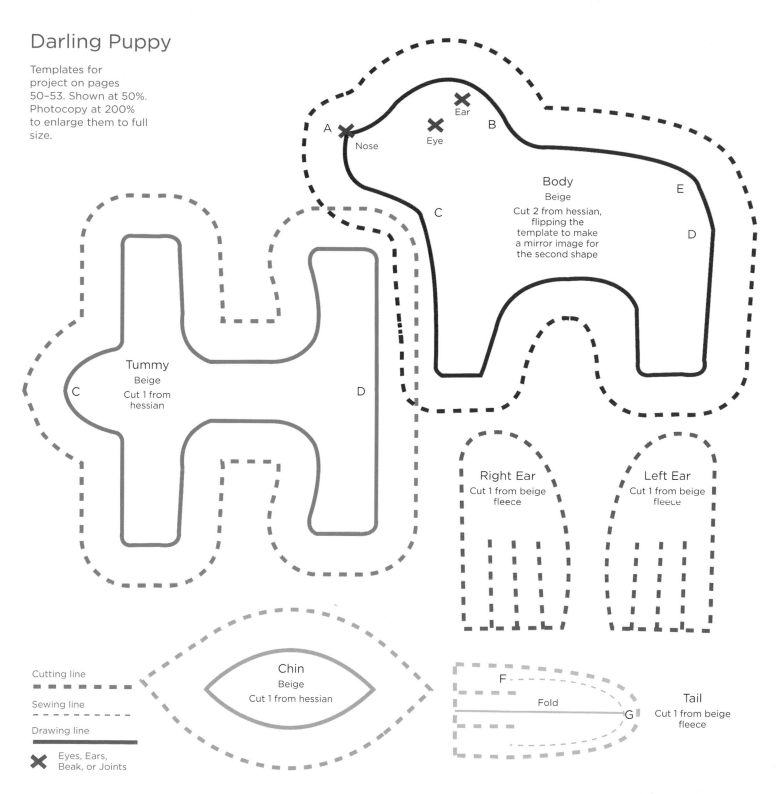

Nose   A

Eye   **Ear**   B

Body
Beige
Cut 2 from hessian, flipping the template to make a mirror image for the second shape

C   D   E

Tummy
Beige
Cut 1 from hessian

C   D

Right Ear
Cut 1 from beige fleece

Left Ear
Cut 1 from beige fleece

Chin
Beige
Cut 1 from hessian

F

Fold   G

Tail
Cut 1 from beige fleece

Cutting line

Sewing line

Drawing line

✕ Eyes, Ears, Beak, or Joints

Floppy Bunny

Templates for project on pages 54–57. Shown at 50%. Photocopy at 200% to enlarge them to full size.

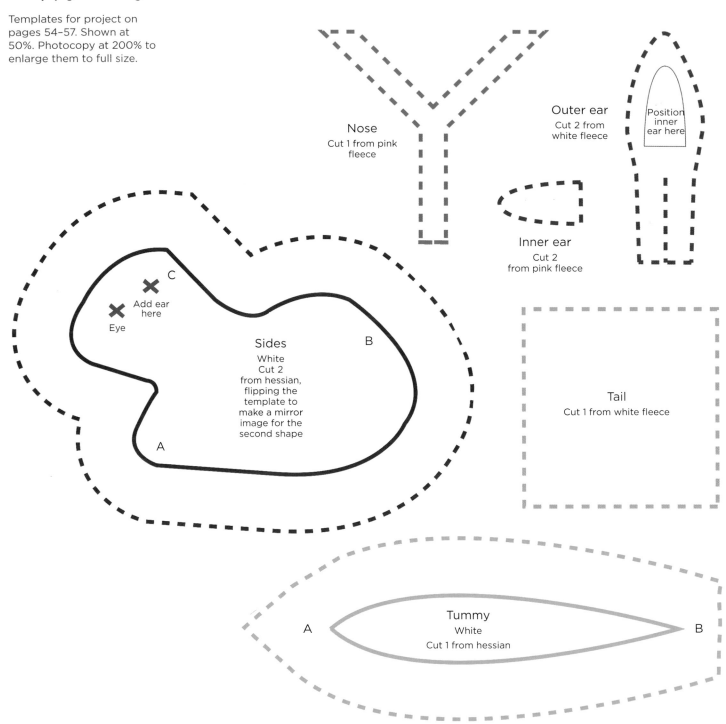

Nose
Cut 1 from pink fleece

Outer ear
Cut 2 from white fleece

Position inner ear here

Inner ear
Cut 2 from pink fleece

C

Add ear here

Eye

Sides
White
Cut 2 from hessian, flipping the template to make a mirror image for the second shape

B

A

Tail
Cut 1 from white fleece

A

Tummy
White
Cut 1 from hessian

B

Tiny Tortoise

Templates for
project on pages
58–61. Shown at 50%.
Photocopy at 200%
to enlarge them to
full size.

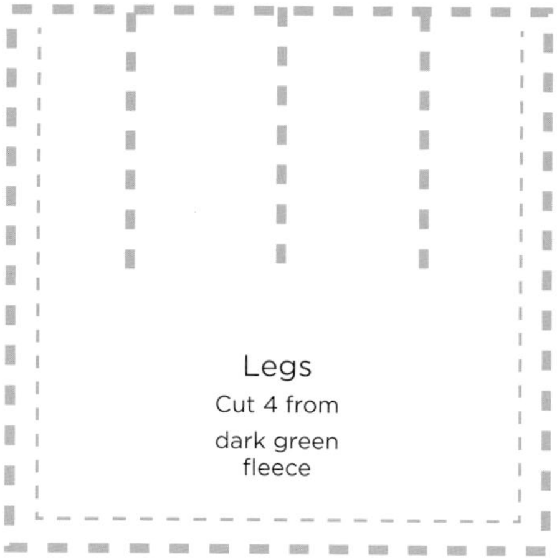

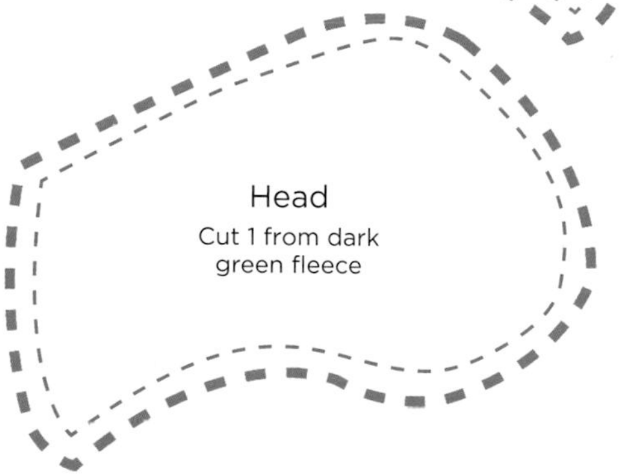

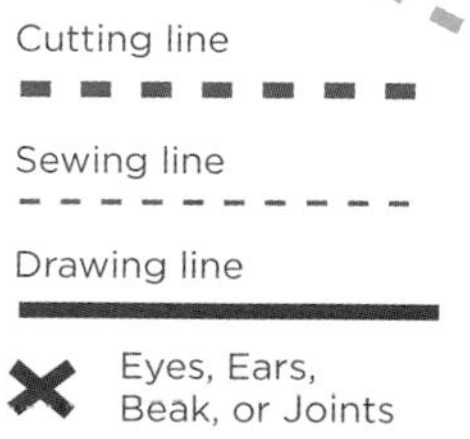

Legs
Cut 4 from
dark green
fleece

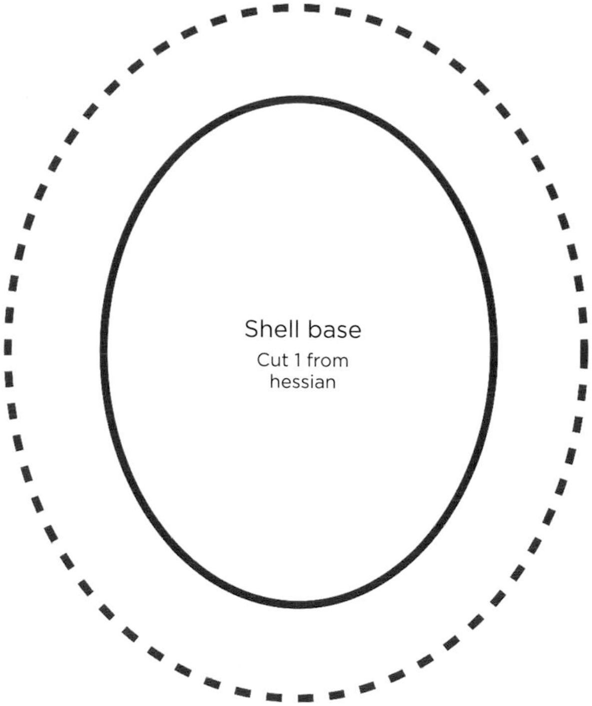

Shell base
Cut 1 from
hessian

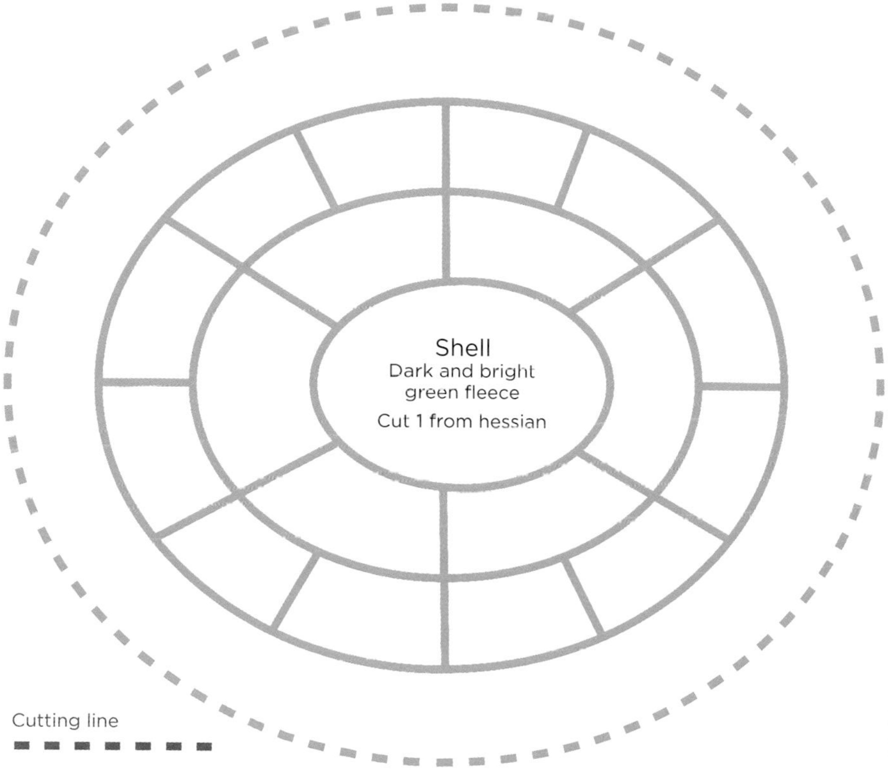

Shell
Dark and bright
green fleece
Cut 1 from hessian

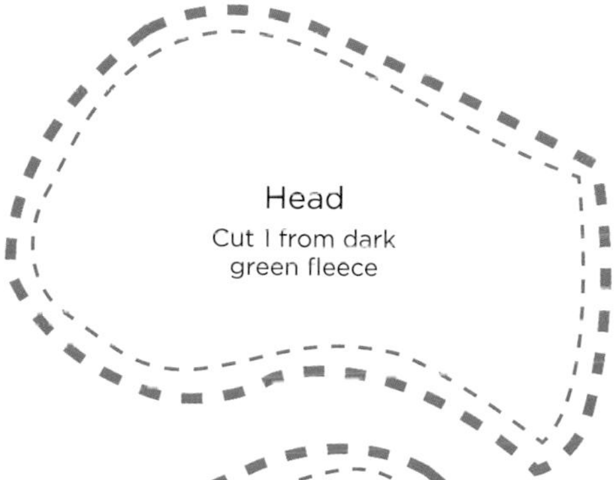

Head
Cut 1 from dark
green fleece

Head
Cut 1 from dark
green fleece

Cutting line

Sewing line

Drawing line

✖ Eyes, Ears,
Beak, or Joints

Pretty Parrot

Templates for project on pages 64–67. Shown at 50%. Photocopy at 200% to enlarge them to full size.

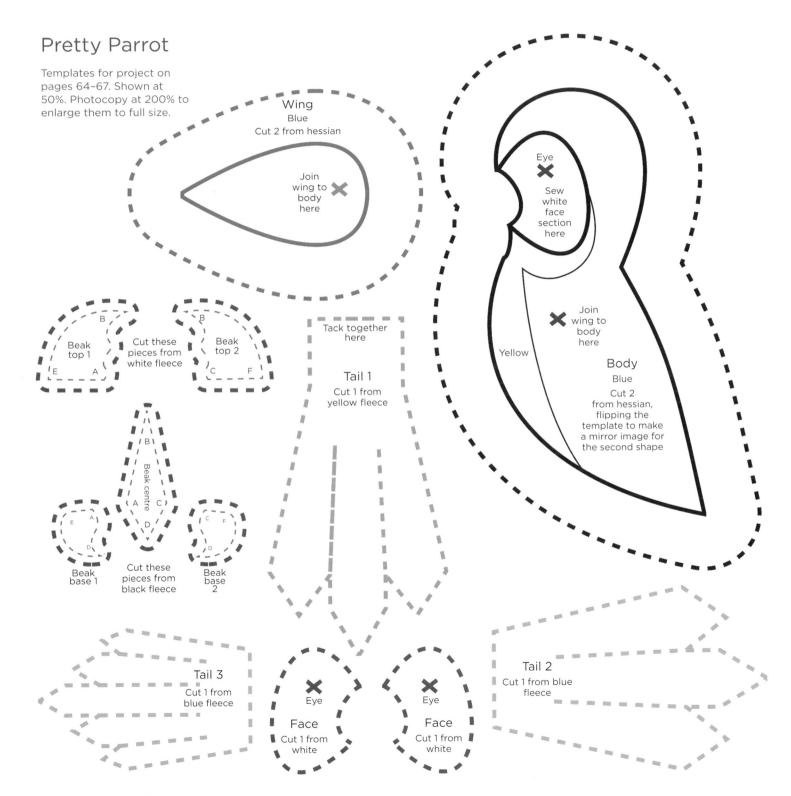

Wing
Blue
Cut 2 from hessian

Join wing to body here

Beak top 1
B
E   A

Cut these pieces from white fleece

Beak top 2
B
C   F

Eye
Sew white face section here

Join wing to body here

Yellow

Body
Blue
Cut 2 from hessian, flipping the template to make a mirror image for the second shape

Beak centre
B
A   C
D

Beak base 1
E   A
D

Cut these pieces from black fleece

Beak base 2
C   F
D

Tack together here

Tail 1
Cut 1 from yellow fleece

Tail 3
Cut 1 from blue fleece

Face
Cut 1 from white
Eye

Face
Cut 1 from white
Eye

Tail 2
Cut 1 from blue fleece

Wise Old Owl

Templates for project on pages 68–71. Shown at 50%. Photocopy at 200% to enlarge them to full size.

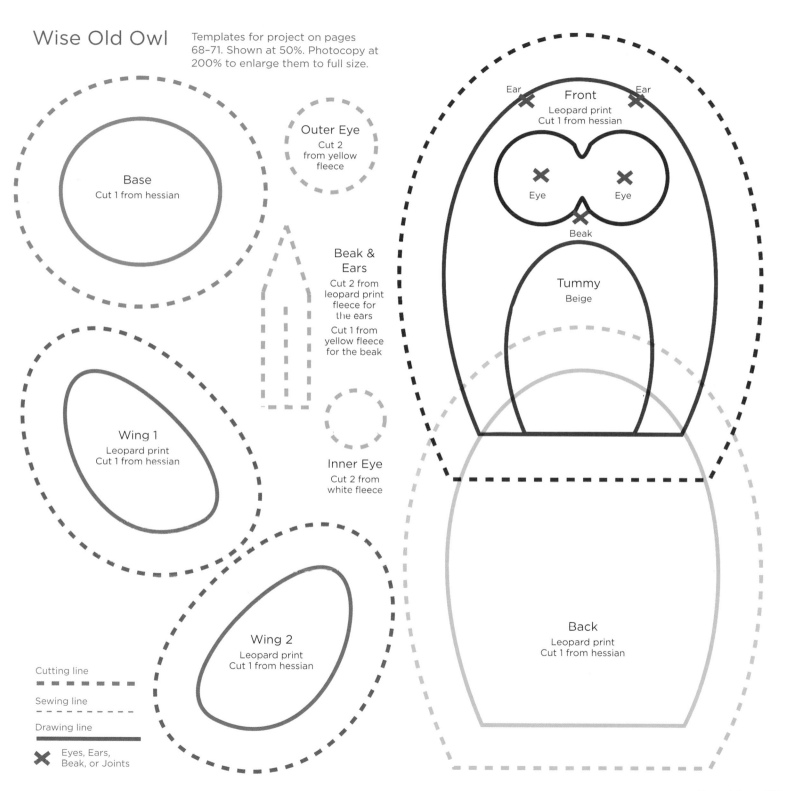

Base
Cut 1 from hessian

Outer Eye
Cut 2 from yellow fleece

Beak & Ears
Cut 2 from leopard print fleece for the ears

Cut 1 from yellow fleece for the beak

Inner Eye
Cut 2 from white fleece

Wing 1
Leopard print
Cut 1 from hessian

Wing 2
Leopard print
Cut 1 from hessian

Ear   **Front**   Ear
Leopard print
Cut 1 from hessian

Eye   Eye

Beak

Tummy
Beige

Back
Leopard print
Cut 1 from hessian

Cutting line

Sewing line

Drawing line

Eyes, Ears, Beak, or Joints

Rockin' Robin

Templates for project on pages 72–75. Shown at 50%. Photocopy at 200% to enlarge them to full size.

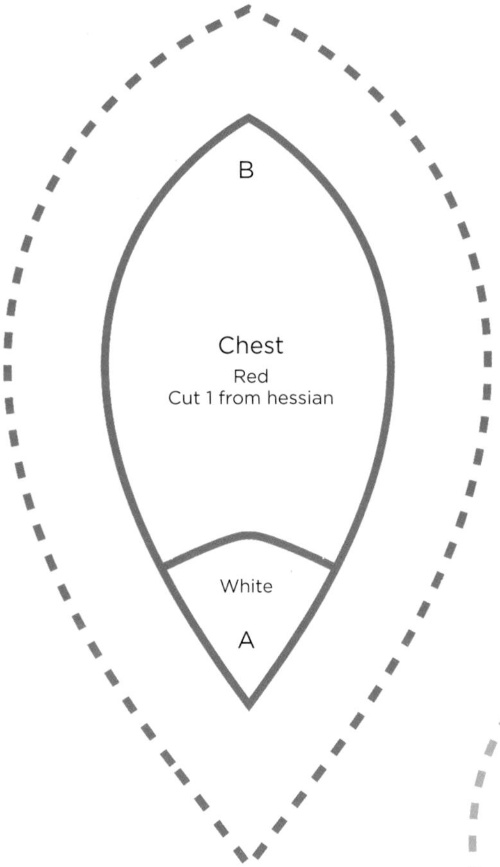

Eye

B
Red

C

Join wing to body here

White

Body
Brown
Cut 2
from hessian,
flipping the
template to make
a mirror image for
the second shape

A

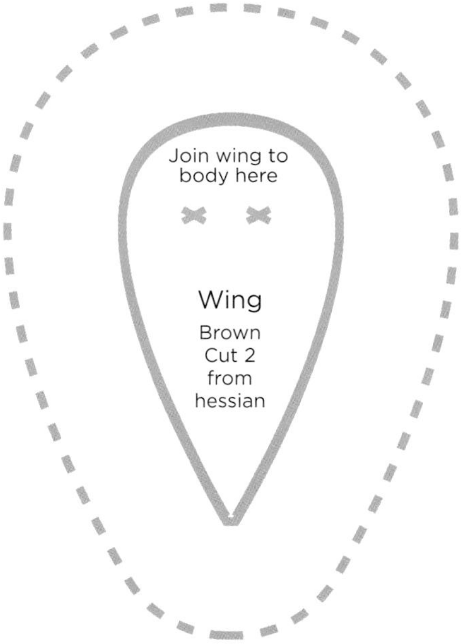

B

Chest
Red
Cut 1 from hessian

White

A

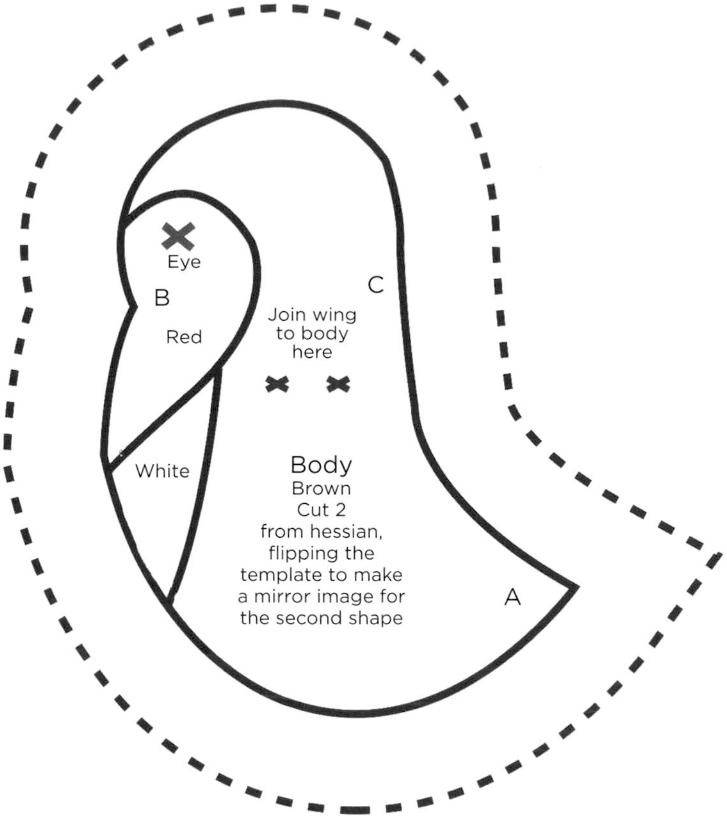

Join wing to body here

Wing
Brown
Cut 2
from
hessian

Beak
Cut 1 from
yellow fleece

Baby Penguin

Templates for project on pages 76–79. Shown at 50%. Photocopy at 200% to enlarge them to full size.

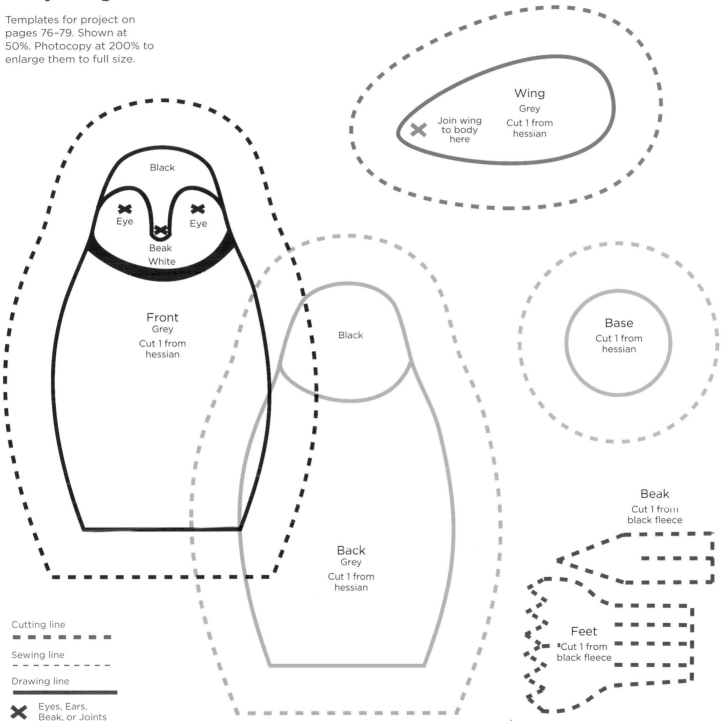

Wing
Grey
Cut 1 from hessian

Join wing to body here

Black

Eye Eye

Beak
White

Front
Grey
Cut 1 from hessian

Black

Base
Cut 1 from hessian

Back
Grey
Cut 1 from hessian

Beak
Cut 1 from black fleece

Feet
Cut 1 from black fleece

Cutting line

Sewing line

Drawing line

Eyes, Ears, Beak, or Joints

Cute Clown Fish

Templates for project on pages 82–85. Shown at 50%. Photocopy at 200% to enlarge them to full size.

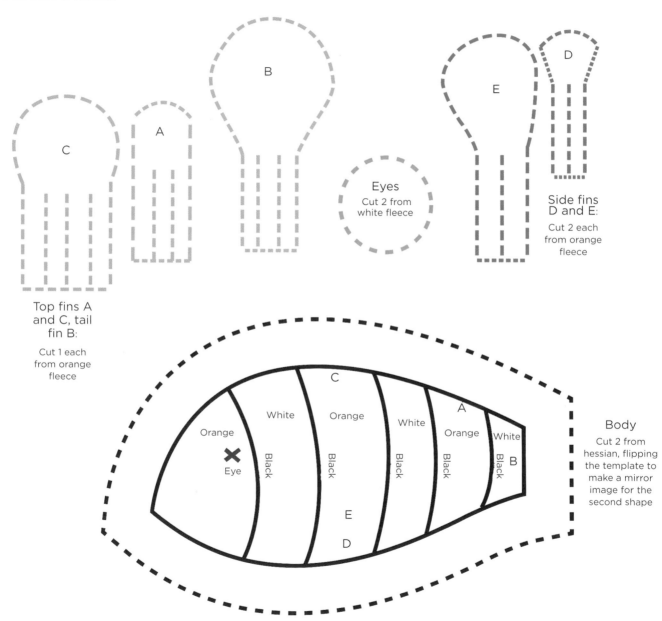

C

A

B

Eyes
Cut 2 from white fleece

E

D

Side fins D and E:
Cut 2 each from orange fleece

Top fins A and C, tail fin B:
Cut 1 each from orange fleece

Orange

White

C

Orange

White

A

Orange

White

B

Black

Black

Black

Black

Black

Eye

E

D

Body
Cut 2 from hessian, flipping the template to make a mirror image for the second shape

Snuggly Seal

Templates for project on pages 86–89. Shown at 50%. Photocopy at 200% to enlarge them to full size.

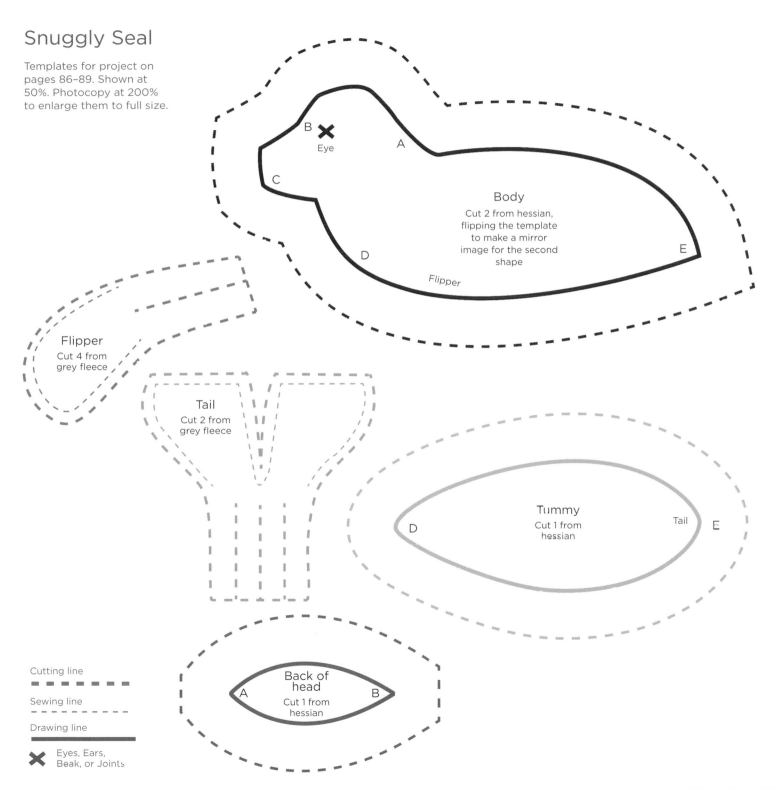

B
✖
Eye

A

C

D

Body
Cut 2 from hessian, flipping the template to make a mirror image for the second shape

E

Flipper

Flipper
Cut 4 from grey fleece

Tail
Cut 2 from grey fleece

Tummy
Cut 1 from hessian

D

Tail

E

Back of head
Cut 1 from hessian

A

B

Cutting line

Sewing line

Drawing line

✖ Eyes, Ears, Beak, or Joints

Flappy Turtle

Templates for project on pages 90–93. Shown at 50%. Photocopy at 200% to enlarge them to full size.

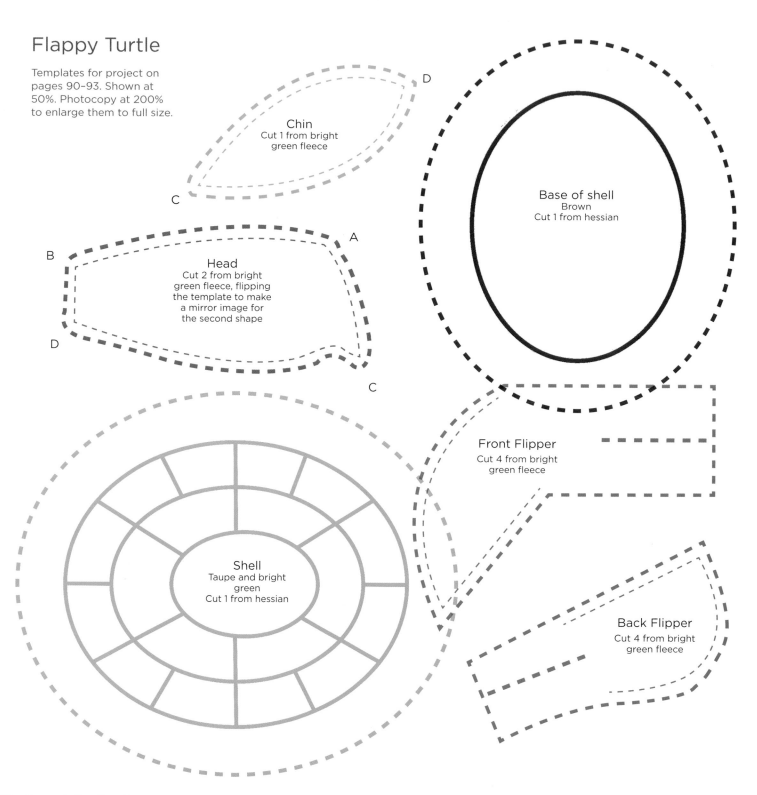

Chin
Cut 1 from bright green fleece

D

C

Base of shell
Brown
Cut 1 from hessian

B

A

Head
Cut 2 from bright green fleece, flipping the template to make a mirror image for the second shape

D

C

Front Flipper
Cut 4 from bright green fleece

Shell
Taupe and bright green
Cut 1 from hessian

Back Flipper
Cut 4 from bright green fleece

Crazy Frog

Templates for project on pages 94–97. Shown at 50%. Photocopy at 200% to enlarge them to full size.

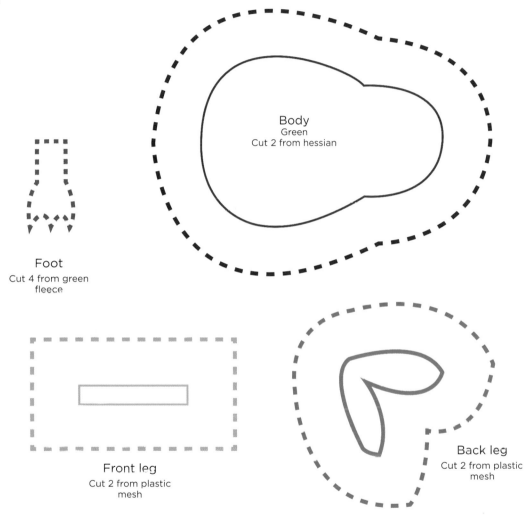

Body
Green
Cut 2 from hessian

Foot
Cut 4 from green fleece

Front leg
Cut 2 from plastic mesh

Back leg
Cut 2 from plastic mesh

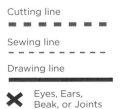

Cutting line

Sewing line

Drawing line

Eyes, Ears, Beak, or Joints

Index

B

Baby Penguin 76–79, 123
backstitch 106
base fabric, see hessian
Big Bold Badger 14–17, 109
bowling pins 75

C

cotton fabrics 99
Crazy Frog 94–97, 127
Cuddly Kitten 46–49, 116
Cute Clown Fish 82–85, 124
cutting out
    hessian and fleece 100, 101
    proggy strips 101
cutting tools 98

D

Darling Puppy 50–53, 117
doorstop 79, 107

E

eyes and noses 99
    inserting 105

F

feet and ears, tying on 105
felt 99
Flappy Turtle 90–93, 126
fleece 99, 101
Floppy Bunny 54–57, 118
Fluffy Duck 40–43, 115
Friendly Fox 10–13, 108

G

glove puppet 71

H

Happy Hedgehog 18–21, 110
hessian 99, 100
    cutting out 100
    joining sections 106
    securing edges of 100, 103
    weaving technique 103
hot water bottle cover 93, 107

L

limbs, tying on 105
Little Lamb 28–31, 112
loop stitch 104

M

making up 106
materials 6, 99
mouse 21

O

oversewing 106

P

cushions 107
Pink Pig 32–35, 113
plastics, recycled 97, 99
Pretty Parrot 64–67, 120
proggy stitch 102
proggy technique 102–103
proggy tool 98

R

resources 107
Rockin' Robin 72–75, 122
rotary cutter and board 98
rugs 6, 107
running stitch 106

S

Sassy Squirrel 22–25, 111
scaling up designs 100
sheep's fleece 99
Snuggly Seal 86–89, 125
Spooky Bat 36–39, 114
stab stitch 106
strip cutter board 98
strip snip tool 98
strips, measuring and cutting 101

T

T-shirt fabrics 99
tea cosy 35, 107
techniques 102–106
templates 108–127
    enlarging and transferring 100–101
Tiny Tortoise 58–61, 119
tools 98

W

walrus 89
weaving technique 103
Wise Old Owl 68–71, 121

Acknowledgements

This book is dedicated to my Nan (grandma) and Auntie Sue, who started me on my crafty journey and taught me to sew. I would also like to thank Sarah, my publisher, for taking a chance on me, and Julie, my editor, who I know had a frustrating time trying to catch me around an increasingly hectic schedule.